90% Human

BY KONRAD NOAH PIERCEY

This book is dedicated to my parents Rodney and Katarzyna Piercey.
Without them, I wouldn't be able to explore this beautiful world.

Contents

CONTENTS

good design is innovative

good design makes a product useful

good design is aesthetic

good design helps us to understand a product

good design is unobtrusive

good design is honest

good design is durable

good design is consequent to the last detail

good design is concerned with the environment

good design is as little design as possible

good design is back to purity, back to simplicity

— Dieter Rams

Introduction

Machine learning (ML) systems can take action on your behalf. These actions, and the reasoning behind them, are often hidden and hard to interpret, difficult even for the creators and designers of said systems.

Current transparency solutions that attempt to disclose what an intelligent system "tracks" or try to describe how a system works do not help maintain users' agency in manipulative system scenarios. In combination with users' dynamic malleability and sensitivity (or lack thereof), while interacting with these systems, problems arise due to the nature and operating parameters of intelligent system design, machine learning specifically.

Defining a set of principles and applied processes that are broadly applicable to users interacting with machine learning systems is the premise of this book. Specifically, highlighting the applicability of principles and processes that impact end-consumer design solutions and business profitability.

Three concepts—educational, simple, intriguing (ESI)—must be "designed" into any consumer software product that integrates high-level ML in systems functionality. Administering these design principles will benefit user's autonomy, agency, and safety—while reducing negative impact on business growth.

The ESI approach can be used in any number of situations. No matter how much ML technologies might change or improve, ESI will remain valid and useable across many domains, applicable for the next 25 years.

SHAPING USERS

Can a simple application make you feel cold? Drive fast? Eat more? Listen to louder music? These are the subtle effects of ML systems. Proven over 10 years of academic research, intelligent systems have shown a resounding capability for covert influence, which can lead to negative side effects for both the users of such systems and the businesses operating them.

This book will explore how these consequences are connected, the research behind them, and how real designers can make a positive impact and, in doing so, protect users and improve the profitability and sustainability of their companies.

DEFINITIONS

- **Machine learning (1959, Author Samuel):** The field of study of giving computers the ability to learn without being explicitly programmed.
- **(Modern) machine learning:** Focuses on developing algorithms capable of identifying patterns within large datasets and making decisions or predictions based on that data.
- **Intelligent machines:** A computational system that can perform tasks requiring cognitive abilities such as learning, reasoning, perception, problem-solving, and decision-making. Such machines often use artificial intelligence techniques, including machine learning, neural networks, and expert systems to adapt to new situations and improve performance over time.
- **Intelligent systems:** A broader concept that includes both hardware and software designed to simulate human intelligence and decision-making processes. Unlike individual intelligent machines, intelligent systems often involve interconnected components like AI models, sensors, and computing frameworks to perceive, analyze, and respond to dynamic environments.
- **(IIS) Interactive Intelligent Systems:** A society of connected agents, or ML systems, where there exists an interactive processes to achieve user goals.
- **Artificial intelligence (AI):** The broad field of creating machines that can perform tasks that typically require human intelligence, such as reasoning, problem-solving, perception, and decision-making.
- **User experience (UX) design:** The building of interfaces with which users interact with a company, including its services and products. UX design is

meant to meet the exact needs of customers without encumbering them with confusion and be a joy to own/use.

- **User interface:** The point of interaction between a user and a device or digital software. It encompasses all the visual elements, controls, and design features that allow users to interact with computers, applications, or websites—including buttons, menus, icons, and layout structures.
- **Useful AI:** Solutions that provide the functions required to satisfy target users' needs in valid-usage scenarios in their work and life.
- **Usable AI:** Solutions that are easy to learn and use via optimal user experience created by effective human-computer interaction (HCI) design.
- **Interpretable AI:** AI systems whose decision-making processes can be understood by humans.

What This Book Is About

90% Human is a design thinking methodology, framework, and mindset. Its contents span a variety of concepts relating to design solutions and integration at scale for machine learning—specifically in consumer products.

WHAT YOU'LL LEARN

Central to this book is not AI products that generate "creative" output (e.g., GPT and LLMs). It's about how the average consumer product is, can, and will be enabled by AI and ML. We will discover foundational principles upon which well-designed ML can be built and explore the effects of such systems on users' perception of the world—and how it is being harmed or healed by current design practices. The book is a mix of design, business, psychology, and philosophy—all deeply rooted in technical know-how.

This book **will not** look at ways users can correct the machine's computational model - instead it looks at the underlaying relationship between user and machine. Identifying ways to create transparency by using information disclosure.

This book does not explore how to use AI to produce design work.

KICKSTARTING YOUR IMAGINATION

Imagine a world where everything—from your toothbrush to your teddy bear—

has been infused with the power of ML. What would that look like? How would that change your relationship with the products you love, care about, and use on a daily basis?

Machine learning, deep learning, and artificial intelligence comprise the fastest-growing tech sectors of the 21st century. By different markers, ML growth is set to exceed $200 billion by 2029. AI could contribute up to $15.7 trillion to the global economy in 2030, more than the current output of China and India combined. Statistics like this are somewhat hard to grasp but what we do know is that the industry is booming and every product and business wants a piece of the pie. By the way, that pie ... is your pie. The data of you and your behavior that businesses have harvested whenever you've been on the internet.

This book is as much about design and machine learning as it is about psychology, business, and the importance of user autonomy. Understanding all this will be a journey. First, to understand the scope of effect of ML and its relevancy to design, which lays the foundation of how to think about ML and its impact. Next is the problem space, with the middle chapters exploring issues related to ML and how it is affecting the products and services we interact with daily. Finally, we will explore solutions to problems in this space, some of which are directly relevant today while others will be explored through the lens of the future and we will go over a new model of training ourselves (and our teams) to think about UX and UI design in the machine learning context.

Within what I refer to as the ESI framework—**educational, simple, intriguing**—outlined later in the book, we will see how design roadmapping is necessary at the start of ML integrations to shift the dynamic from reactive to proactive, one that continually considers the effect of ML on consumers and which must include building new types of products/services which enhance the relationship between users and customers.

To foster better relationships, design will be the natural storytelling medium. Design can no longer be an afterthought in the ML/AI space; it's imperative that we set new standards for user experience thresholds and limitations on what we deem as socially acceptable in current product-design circles. With new examples of products gone wrong popping up year after year—the worst of which include legal action and liability for negligence—company executives and designers can serve not only end users but shareholders by protecting company staff from unnecessary litigation (e.g., Facebook and Google lawsuits on data protection and privacy).

Articulating machine learning is complex. It is a broad topic. There are various ways in which to apply, assess, and train models. Numerous model types and algorithms are joined together, with mixing and matching different ML models now part of an ML engineer and data scientist's toolkit. For designers, this entire field is a new world and there are big questions about what design and product personnel should know about it. What is their role in the grand scheme of integrating this technology?

Machine learning uses several methods to try and predict output or assign values to a set(s) of data. Input and output—this is the foundation of all things ML. For designers and product professionals, it's important to understand that the core nature of ML is this balance—input and output—and how/what you choose to put in influences how it is screened and the ultimate form of the output "solution." Most importantly, how success is defined is crucial.

All of these are key necessities for great ML design, where we must bridge the gaps between computer science, data, business, and user experience. This is where the magic happens, the creation of the best product experience through the integration of ML and AI in a useful, organic way. Meeting these necessities allows designers to create a comprehensive framework of ownership and responsibility within an organization.

The concepts for a machine's input and output form the bedrock upon which all other aspects of the system are built. These foundational elements, coupled with clearly defined success parameters, allow designers to create a comprehensive framework of ownership and responsibility within an organization. Understanding what attributes a model is intaking is crucial, as it sets the stage for realizing both the positive and negative effects of AI/ML integration.

For ML experts and technical stakeholders, defining success parameters is of extreme importance. These not only guide the development and refinement of the model but also establish benchmarks for evaluating performance. Success in ML is typically multifaceted, encompassing both technical metrics and broader business and user-centric outcomes. Technical success is often measured in terms of model accuracy, precision, recall, and other performance metrics. These are crucial for assessing how well the model performs its designated tasks. However, a technically high-performing model does not necessarily translate to user satisfaction or business success.

Successful ML integration requires a holistic approach that balances technical accuracy, user satisfaction, and business objectives. This is a collaborative effort involving engineers, data scientists, UX/UI designers, and business strategists. Each stakeholder plays a vital role in shaping the model's development and ensuring it meets the defined success criteria. A thorough understanding of these components allows organizations to anticipate and mitigate potential impacts, both positive and negative.

By defining clear success parameters encompassing technical, user, and business dimensions, stakeholders can create robust ML systems that drive innovation and deliver meaningful value.

A QUICK NOTE ON ETHICS

Constant, ongoing, forever changing.

This is machine learning.

And also true of human nature. The ESI design principles go beyond immediate need. Instead, they try to create a dialogue between the system and users, allowing for adaptation to the changing societal and individual dynamics of humankind and each user. **Therefore, to derive success criteria from ethics would be creating a point of failure.**

That being said, we should give notice to some prominent coverage of this topic.

> Because of their nature, the full benefit of these technologies will be attained only if they are aligned with society's defined values and ethical principles. Through this work we intend, therefore, to establish frameworks to guide and inform dialogue and debate around the non-technical implications of these technologies, in particular related to ethical aspects. We understand "ethical" to go beyond moral constructs and include social fairness, environmental sustainability, and our desire for self-determination. (Institute of Electrical and Electronics Engineers, 2019)

Introduction

The major challenge of including ethical criteria in product design can be understood as an attempt to solve ML-related issues by prescribing one solution as the methodology for "ethical machines." Unfortunately, society's ethical values do not remain constant; they are forever changing and evolving, just like AI.

A simpler approach might be useful—To demonstrate the ongoing evolution of a machine's understanding of a user and their interaction with it. Only at this level of transparency can users hope to correct machines when those systems stray from the line of reasoning or actioning that is not desired. Only by noticing the effect a machine is having on them might users realize that ethical & value alignment actions are required.

THOUGHT EXPERIMENT

For example, in the early 1970s, the average middle-class working family viewed strict drug enforcement policies as correct, ethical, and morally justified. Incarcerating someone for over a decade for the possession of 16 ounces of marijuana was viewed as the "right" thing to do. As of 2024, this opinion has been displaced by more divergent ethical norms. Approximately 68 percent of Americans now believe that marijuana should be legalized, reflecting a significant shift in societal attitudes toward drug policy. "Right" and "wrong" changed (Pew Research Center, 2024).

If modern-day intelligent agents were accessible in the 1970s, what might be their "ethical" behavior in service to a function? How might the machine make assumptions and interpretations from the 70s hardline drug approach? What actions might it take if used in that societal environment? Imagine a recommendation model for jail sentences used by a judge to inform decision-making on punishment.

What is the ethically correct solution to questions involving reproductive rights like abortion? Or euthanasia and assisted suicide? Who should be deciding how the machine interprets these concepts and uses them in decision-making or performing tangential discreet actions?

There are many "common sense" ethical design choices designers can adhere to; none of them are fully encompassing, easily adopted, or favored simultaneously by shareholders and various demographic groups around the world.

An Inorganic Relationship

What drives humans? What drives machines?

A machine should be logical; humans, famously, are not.

To bridge the growing gap between the two, human and machine, humans must understand the fault in the machine, which is its inability to self-audit when things go wrong, when the machine acts against the intent and preferences of end users. Current AI systems lack the sort of self-awareness capacities that humans might expect from another human colleague.

How is the user experience affected by machine learning? Through the lens of *action* and *information*, we can gain a new way of visualizing this relationship.

As a user, you can take action on the machine while also consuming information. Action and information. The entirety of UX can be separated into either of these verticals. With the introduction of highly efficient ML technologies, specifically reinforcement learning (RL) techniques, **action and information initiate a conversation between the machine and the human,** a symbiotic one between organic and inorganic. As it occurs, output from either machine or user, and responses from either side, trigger a hidden dance, which occurs as we interact with ML-powered software.

The machine learns from the user, customizing the content or controls of the interface. Users learn based on what the machine chooses to show the user—a button here, a video there. These concepts are known as choice architecture, which is a means of limiting or adapting the actions and information available to users. It is deeply linked to the ability of machines to covertly influence consumers.

A new form of feedback is born, manifesting in indirect control. Not to be confused with LLMs—where users directly talk in their natural language with the software, this new relationship with machines is more discreet. ML models seek to bridge the growing gap between the two, human and machine. Humans must understand the fault in the machine, which is its inability to self-audit when things go wrong, when the machine acts against the intent and preferences of end users. Current AI systems lack the sort of self-awareness capacities that humans might expect from another human colleague.

*FOOTNOTE: Choice architecture first emerged with Richard Thaler and Cass Sunstein's 2008 book, *Nudge: Improving Decisions about Health, Wealth, and Happiness*. Thaler coined the term choice architecture to describe how insights from behavioral economics could be used to influence choices, without changing their objective values (Thaler and Sunstein, 2008).

An Inorganic Relationship

Mental models are the backbone of this misalignment between the user and the machine. This is where the hidden layer exists. Via this opaque landscape, one without clear boundaries or markers, machines can deceive users. Lauren Willis's 2020 paper "Deception By Design" explains this in detail (Willis, 2020). Deception by machines is inevitable and a very pertinent issue to resolve. In 2016, Facebook faced the music (Lauer, 2021) as a plethora of fake news affected real elections in the United States. Articles reinforcing users' perceptions of their political views (filter bubbles) spread and served users politically motivated material from international antagonists (i.e., Russia). Neither the media feed from the Kremlin, nor the loop of confirmation bias, was wanted by most Facebook users, yet that is what the apps were trained to do—serve users information they appeared to thirst for.

Another example of machine deception is video streaming platforms. Have you ever wondered why watching content online seems more addictive? Ever binged a show on streaming platforms like Netflix or YouTube? These and similar streaming platforms use ML to suggest shows and content that users are likely to engage with. This helps generate revenue for the company by creating repetitive product<>user interactions.

Take Pavlov's dog. In this most famous experiment, Pavlov taught his dog to salivate at the sound of a chime. This special learning method trained the dog to expect food when hearing the sound. Our apps work in a similar fashion. As we interact with Netflix, Spotify, or Facebook, they learn from us. When we pop open the app and click on an icon, we're having a conversation with the machine. That "conversation" provides customers with improved suggestions but also the danger of polarizing content. Because inherent in our interaction with machines is their ability to serve us content and perform actions, a Pavlovian chime is triggered—these online services are now mutant forms of Pavlov's original experiment.

*FOOTNOTE: Although supervised learning—particularly linear regression—is among today's most widely used ML methods, some of the larger issues relating to ML are seeded from continuous learning systems like those used in reinforcement learning. RL is more influential due to its ability to morph and adapt without screening from engineers or designers of the system. Output is under a less controlled environment. Many of the largest ML models for consumer products are based on reinforcement learning.

Probably he would have never imagined his work used in this way. The super-engineered leveraging of humans' natural tendencies to engage with things to "make us salivate" for more content. The machine serves us what we want in order to solve its goals, and its goal is getting the doggy chow (i.e., making us click, watch, and listen). These are called success metrics in business practices (Carroll et al., 2021). When the machine successfully shows us something we engage with, the machine is served a kind of digital treat, rewarded for making us click.

A path towards solving the ensuing dilemma—the souring relationship between humans and machines—we must answer the question "Who, why, and how are success metrics determined to reward the machine?"

> The tools we use, and how we use them, are changing. Or, as John Culkin noted in 1967, "We shape our tools and, thereafter, our tools shape us" (Culkin, 1967).

The rate of change in these tools and their ability to mold each of us presents unfounded potential, but also a darker path. A major risk is that users miscalculate how to appropriately use them. Like a caveman with a chainsaw, a user might harm themselves, unaware of the limitations or repercussions of using the tool. Fast forward to a world where most digital tools are now super-powered with intelligent system mechanics (e.g., machine learning). The benefits and risks are both astounding.

What happens when a tool has a mind of its own? Making decisions on your behalf—for you—which you might not even be aware of.

UX builds a relationship between human and machine. UX is a story-telling mechanism of interaction between these two forces. Designers relate this to bridging the gap, making human and machine seamless in their connection.

In the early years, at the inception of user experience design, the goal was to make human-computer experiences more natural.

The effort was kicked off from the space of ergonomics, going back to the ancient Greeks. This was before the era of personal computing devices.

The design industry had its sights on correcting poorly designed machines or systems that were clunky and complex; one of the first modern applications of ergonomics was a quest for workplace efficiency. Toyota developed its famous human-centered production system (Eren, 2024) which, at its core, was meant to create experiences that felt more natural—more human in their operation. This optimization would increase worker effectiveness. A later journey led to human-computer interaction (HCI). Many of the most influential developments came out of Xerox's PARC (Palo Alto Research Center), such as the graphical user interface and the mouse.

Great HCI, and the resultant user experiences, are a conversation. As it is with conversing between living beings, there are good conversations and those we'd rather not have had. The "conversation" we have with our tools and products has an ideal state. The most comfortable state, which most users seek, will be similar to the tools and products they've interacted with before. The expectation i s that our interaction with tools and products is natural, built upon previous relationships with the products we've already had time to adapt to. In design industries, we call these affordances, which include both perceived and actual functions. Users never approach a new tool or service with zero expectations. There will always be mental model associations from previous interactions with similar equipment or tools.

Users have a constant and ongoing relationship with everything. From the implements in their tool belt (hammer and chisel) to tasks completed using sophisticated software (email and Photoshop). Users of physical or digital tools form relationships and associations as soon as they make contact with a product.

Whether a tool is used for a few seconds or many years, users develop expectations about how it should work based on its design, behavior, and response to input. Consider how slowly most people have embraced virtual reality. This technology requires a completely new way of interacting. Now, think about the transition from using paper and pencil to typing on a modern QWERTY keyboard, which was introduced around 1878. This change was significant, yet now just as simple as mastering a basic tool like a screwdriver.

Historically, tools like screwdrivers, paper and pencil, or keyboards have had a consistent function. **They didn't adapt or change their purpose for each user.** A screwdriver didn't become a different tool for each person who used it, nor did paper and pencil offer different features or change their physical attributes for different writers. These tools remained unchanged, no matter who used them. This consistency is what made these products reliable and trustworthy throughout their use.

Now, the relationship between human and machine has changed. No longer does the tool or product produce the same response for each user.

Digital products have the ability to morph and change after each use.

In the ever-evolving landscape of digital products, a remarkable transformation is underway. Our AI-driven tools, once perceived as uniform and monolithic, now possess the remarkable ability to tailor unique output in each instance—while maintaining their collective identity. This paradigm shift challenges traditional notions of design and user experience, prompting us to rewrite the instruction manual for navigating this new frontier. How do we design for it?

Intelligent machine responses, though part of a larger whole, possess an inherent dynamism—an ability to adapt, evolve, and resonate with individual users. No longer confined to rigid templates, our digital products now weave intricate narratives by responding to context, tone, action, and inaction.

With some ML systems, as users continue to engage with the software, they encounter a delightful paradox: the more they interact, the more personalized the experience becomes as the machine's model expands and trains. Each query, each prompt, contributes to a rich tapestry that solidifies the user's "identity" within the system. A machine learning system learns, refines, and crafts bespoke outputs that reflect the user's nuances. No screwdriver or typewriter ever had such superpowers.

Modern AI researchers argue for a move away from anthropomorphizing AI, as opposed to the public heavily associating human-like qualities with AI products (Deshpande et al., 2023). On the other hand, for software creators, there's an argument for the opposite approach, of embracing the humanizing functionality of these new tools and services. From that vantage point, we might begin to fully understand how to design for the relationship now developing between AI products and users.

As we rewrite the instruction manual, let's celebrate the delicate dance between uniformity and uniqueness. This is both a power and a threat. In UX, there exists a core principle: Always allow the user to maintain a sense of control over the product (Norman, 2013). But there exists no principle to account for products with dynamic responses that harbor personality or intent. Products have personalities, and they cater differently to each one of us.

Creating safe tools and products once started with laborious manuals and training. Now we are entering a new domain where the concept of instructions is opaque. Is it feasible to have instruction manuals for products with dynamic personalities?

An Inorganic Relationship

The origin of UX in HCI was crafting the user experience based on fixed points in the product experience, where the user and machine met to exchange information, or produce a set of responses/ actions, as the basis of the relationship.

What if these anchor points of machine-user interaction were never fixed in one place? What if system responses could not be easily reproduced? What if they were constantly changing, constantly shifting? How would our relationship with these same tools and products change? If the output of our products, tools, and services is not consistent, if the variability of system/computer response is infinite and constantly molded to each human, how can we design for a safe user experience?

The answer is information sharing and education. Sharing information on what the system is doing and why—better known as transparency and system monitoring. Also, educating humans on how they are changing the machine and how the machine is changing them. As designers, project managers, or engineers, we must design unique safeguards that embrace the concept of dynamism in product uniqueness (a unique product experience for each user), meaning **products with personalities**.

A Conversation Between Product and User

Both parties are capable of achieving positive outcomes with the right support. We must imagine this latent space where intelligent systems and users connect—while also realizing how they are separated. Though it may be hard for the average person to detect, our digital partners are conversing with us, understanding what we like to do, and finding ways to best support that. This is the beauty of machine learning—it's discreetness. However, like all powerfully disruptive technologies, we need to realize how these systems influence us. How they mold our thoughts and behaviors. Just like any relationship with a tool or product, though in this case, the product has greater autonomy to provide real-time adjustments to how it responds to the user. ML systems are dynamic and pliable in contrast to the digital systems for which traditional UX design was developed.

Machines can categorize and assign quantitative values to topics that humans don't naturally relate to numeric scales. This translation of humanistic qualities into percentages and decimals presents unique challenges. It disguises human traits as something more measurable. Classification—a common machine learning method for interpreting the world and making sense of inputs—is part of this process. Although AI and ML are often considered neutral, objective, and technical systems, they should not be described so simply. These systems do judge. They have preferences, and the decisions they make are personal.

Designers must relinquish some user-interaction theory concepts and adapt to the new technological landscapes. Designers must think about how to make the invisible nature of relationships quantifiable and visualizable and must understand the inherent dynamism of the user<>system adaptation that ML gives rise to. Through this lens, we can build solutions that drive growth for customers and businesses. Increasing the knowledge of how users converse with machines, and how machines interpret those "conversations" (touch points). This is where solutions lay.

Intelligent systems can quietly learn and adapt to user behavior. Through that medium, these same systems shape user thoughts and behaviors with real-time adjustments to the interfaces we all interact with. Because of this, we must strive to **make the invisible visible**.

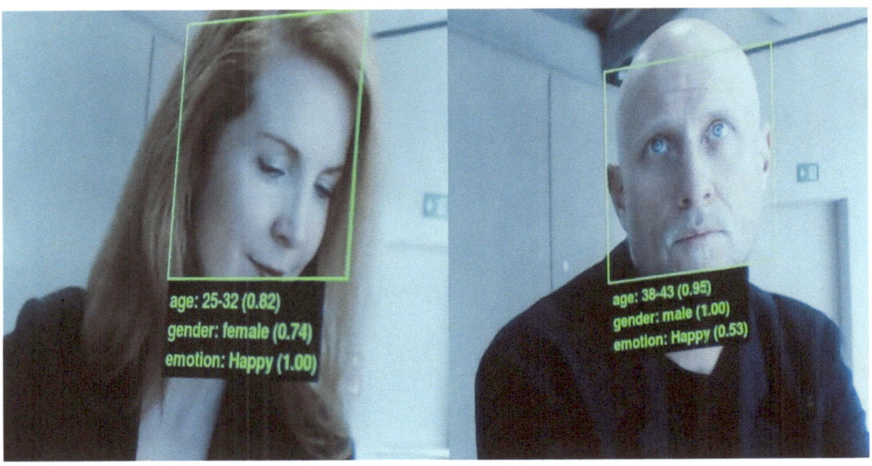

Figure 1: Kate Crawford and Trevor Paglen, Training Humans Installation

A New World Order

Machine learning is a branch of artificial intelligence that uses algorithms to detect patterns in data, then perform tasks based on those patterns. ML algorithms are often used to automate tasks and personalize user experiences, such as providing tailored content and advertisements. They are also used in many cases to analyze user behavior and improve user experiences, identify user preferences, and make predictions.

A New World Order

ML is already saturating our interactions in all domains and with all types of technologies.

- Healthcare
  - Analyzing large-scale medical data to detect early signs of diseases like cancer—often with higher accuracy than human doctors.
  - Accelerating drug discovery by identifying potential compounds and predicting interactions with the human body.
  - Supporting public health by tracking disease outbreaks and forecasting their spread, enabling early intervention.
- Transportation
  - Powering self-driving cars, helping to interpret surroundings, recognizing obstacles, and making real-time decisions.
  - Improving city traffic management by optimizing signal timings, reducing congestion, and cutting emissions.
  - Enhancing aviation through predictive maintenance, identifying issues before failures occur.

THE "PROBLEM"

There is a desire to experience products that are tailor-made for us. Products that act like that coffee shop on the corner where they not only know your name but if you want sugar and crème in your coffee.

As users, we are driven to this ideal. Products and services that know us by name and treat our interaction as uniquely as our local barista. It's only natural to want products that seem to know us and understand us—experiences that are specific, tailored, bespoke.

This is the human condition at work; we can't help but seek this type of interaction with our products or the people we're close to. We want this type of experience not only because it is emotionally satisfying but also because it delivers the best product experiences.

Starting in the second half of the 21st century, most of our digital products will be driven by big data. This will have consequences, like Facebook's fake news issues or overconfidence in Tesla Autopilot (National Highway Traffic Safety Administration, 2024) that we already face. Design will be the overlapping integrator, bridging the gap left by big data and ML. UX and UI design will drive new forces into the domain and broaden our perspective on what we expect from these systems, products, and services that are built on the foundation of big data.

New AI-design standards, which have rapidly matured, are the outcome of a void in the industry's toolkits, driven purely by a need to deliver better system recognition, meaning user awareness of the inner workings of novel technologies like ML, AI, and natural language processing (NLP).

The growth of ML and AI is scaling at rates so fast that it is hard to comprehend. The influence of the domain on our daily lives is all-encompassing, from smartphones to email spam filters. These systems move too fast for us to understand in real time how they might positively or negatively impact our lives.

Both **information** and **action** share a direct line of sight into the two main segments of UX and UI design. All designed things can be grouped into these two categories; basically, how we ingest or consume information and how we interact or take action. The fundamental limitations related to ML/AI integrations and user experiences fall into either one of these categories. The later chapter "Action and Information" dives deeper into this.

Data privacy and disclosure, habit formation and over-reliance—these tendrils link all the critical issues in the burgeoning field of ML design. We see some of these problems today in our social media, marketplaces, and even tangible goods. All are grounded in reality and the trajectory of current consumer and business needs.

How can we format a new level of understanding in the field of product design to account for new issues tied to technological progress? How can we set a bar for minimum acceptability regarding best design practices in ML integration to enable **transparency** and **user agency**?

Biases, the black box effect, and the simplistic nature of echo chambers all stem from systems designed without considering the impact of human-intelligent system interactions. These issues are created by inaccurately separating user needs and business needs. Our relationships with our products will become indistinguishable and we won't know where the product (the AI) decisions end and our interaction (agency) starts; the gaps between system and user are fast vanishing.

What is coming is a world where information is not equal, but bespoke, a world that is presented to us exactly how we want and how we wish to see it (filter bubbles). Is that truly a success? Ethics can lead us toward a step in the right direction but ethical standards are not equal among differing populations and diverging demographics.

How might we grasp the weight of these new thinking systems that offer so much potential and empowering opportunities? We know we must adapt and take advantage of the new landscape of technology, but how? How can we afford to capitalize on the many benefits and efficiencies of ML and AI, all whilst not losing the thing that makes us human—our agency?

*FOOTNOTE: Agency refers to the degree of control, autonomy, and decision-making power that a user has when interacting with an intelligent system. It is a critical concept because AI-driven systems often make decisions on behalf of users, and the way those decisions are presented—or the extent to which users can influence them—impacts user trust, satisfaction, and overall experience.

Deteriorating UX Fundamentals

Why are fundamental UX design principles losing their grip?

Rewind to 1995, when the term UX was just invented. Soon thereafter, 1997 witnessed IBM's Deep Blue, a chess-playing computer that beat the human world champion using a system based fundamentally on machine learning. During this time, software design was shifting. With the introduction and focused application of user experience design principles, complicated software would become much more accessible to the average consumer.

But decades later, an interesting result has become apparent. The interface and the underlying mechanics of software slowly became invisible. Everything from dashboards to desktops were neatly compressing and nesting extraneous and unnecessary controls of the system. This design approach focused on ease of comprehension, ease of use, and of course simplicity—leading to a renaissance for the whole industry.

Figure 2: Sony and Apple TV Remote (Design eats technology.)

Figure 3: NASA's Apollo 11 Mission Control Room

For example, in 1969 our expectations for these systems and our connections with the tools were wildly different from today's handhelds. At that time the term computer meant hardware that sometimes took up an entire room and UI of physical knobs and switches.

A lot can be captured in the simple phrase "less is more." But what does it mean? The Bauhaus movement in Germany (an architectural approach to buildings, spaces, and structural design) was a big driver for new "user-focused" design philosophies. Architecture always had a lot of influence on the digital design industry, but the Bauhaus style directly improved and simplified the movement of bodies through a physical space. UX would use the same approach, seeking to optimize a user's flow through digital space. Uncoincidentally, both Bauhaus and UX embrace the adage "form meets function."

Apart from the many types of stylistic choices available (Bauhaus minimalism, skeuomorphism, brutalism, etc.), it was the shift in content design that arguably led to the minimizing of the modern UI. In the age of content, digital user interfaces were to take a back seat. The UI would be less pivotal in helping users achieve tasks. This translated into fewer buttons and cleaning up the surface of the software. Fast forwarding to 2024, content is still at the top of the stack, now more important than ever. Most modern consumer software services, which rely on leveraging a form of content (specifically, dynamic content) are market leaders. Think Twitter (X), Uber, GrabFood, Spotify, and Netflix.

UX designers have a relentless and ceaseless challenge to "simplify" the interface. It's part of every job. Even if not directly part of the job description or company mission statement, this is what designers strive towards. Simple is easy; simple is clean; simple is elegant. In the wonderful book *Simplicity: A Matter Of Design* by Per Mollerup (2015), simplicity is described in both space and time. As Mollerup signals, interfaces that hide the complexity through overly simplistic design make a trade-off.

Simpler on the surface can lead to complexity in task duration. Restated, it would take more time to complete the task of flying a jumbo jet if one thousand controls were all on a single tablet display. On the other hand, interfaces that surface their operational complexity (i.e., more buttons) sacrifice visual simplicity. For users, this would mean less time to complete the task because all the functions are visible and not hidden behind endless menus. The simplicity concept of a clean interface might be easier for a novice to use (such as a poor passenger in a movie who has

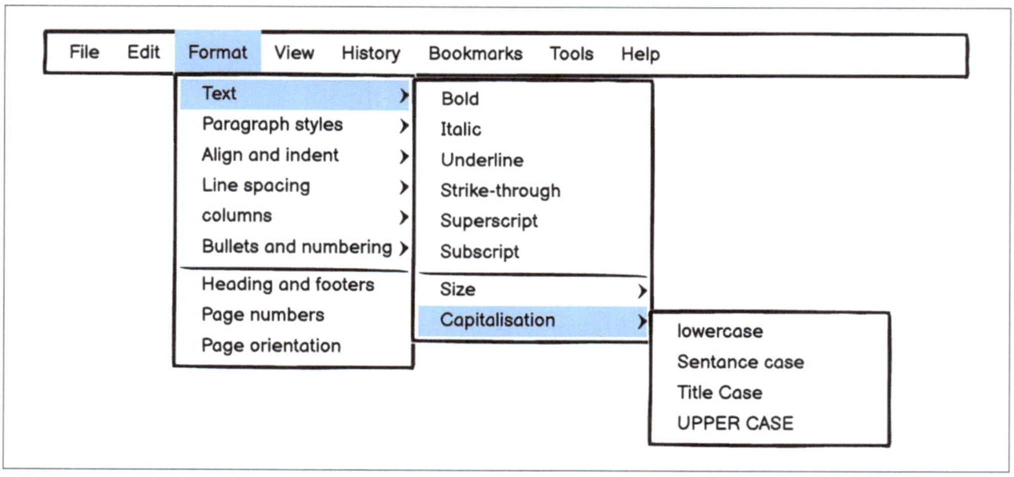

Figure 4: Nested Menus (How system structures can become invisible/visible.)

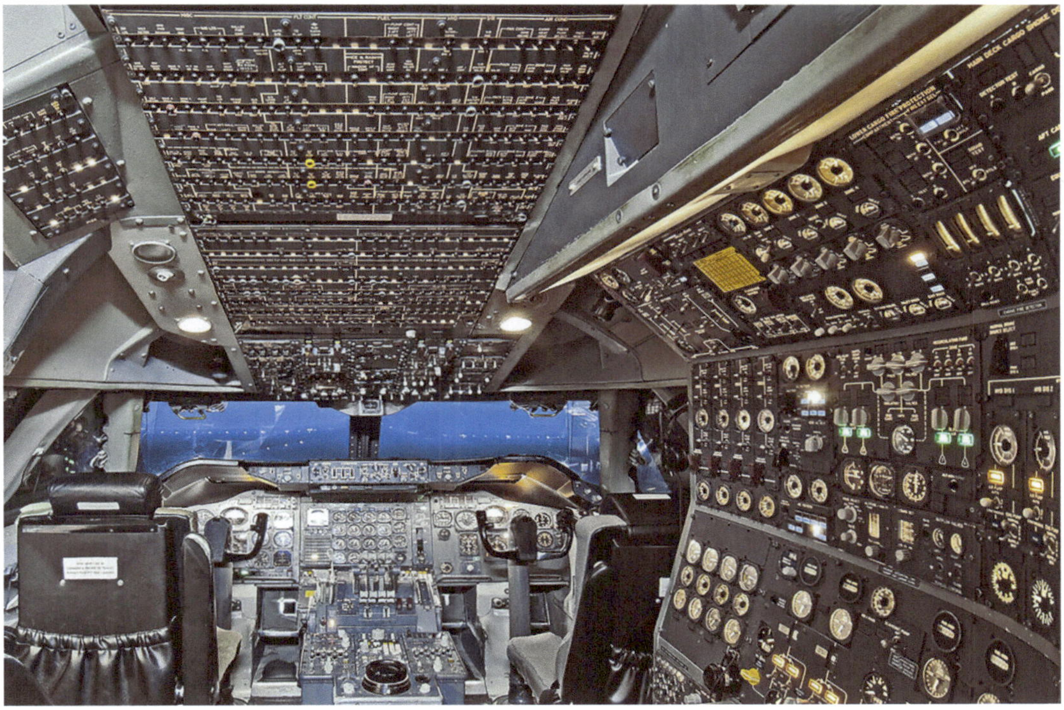

Figure 5: Boeing 747 Flight Deck

to fly the plane after the pilots have been incapacitated) but would make it more complex for real pilots because it would take them longer to access and edit multiple controls at once.

Imagine all the controls and buttons of a modern aircraft's flight deck being removed and replaced with only a single iPad for the display and control of the aircraft. This is design for "complexity in space" rather than "simplicity in time" for task completion.

When a designer is tasked with making the software interface "simple," many unspoken principles of UX are levied. Also referred to as heuristics, these principles include:

- **Visibility of system status:** Design should always keep users informed about what is going on, through appropriate feedback within a reasonable amount of time (Norman, 2013).
- **Consistency and standards:** Users should not be confused about whether different words, situations, or actions mean something different when displayed elsewhere in the system. Don't maintain five different ways of depicting a favorite (heart) button. Users should see the same text and icon everywhere to make it simpler to use.

Both the above principles have been disrupted by the interjection of ML.

These principles are often weighed against other factors, like how the business is structured for revenue generation or how users should perceive the brand identity of the product and service. Should it be like McDonalds—fun, cheap, and everywhere? Or more bespoke, trendy, and expensive like Prada? These questions all go into the thinking of a designer as they try to paint the perfect canvas of interactivity between the user and software. Some businesses might leverage a single sale as their main moneymaker. Think automotive ownership. On the other hand, there's the infamous subscription model of music and video streaming applications, like Netflix and Apple Music. These models try to get the user to engage consistently to ensure they stick with the platform. Lastly, there are freemium models, a more modern approach to growing a user base. The idea is to activate initial users with a free but limited service, then leverage paywalled and expanded functionality by identifying the most popular features that users demand.

But currently, in the mix of factors designers weigh, simplicity rules them all. This steadfast concept still holds sway in modern tech companies that were built for a different era, one of static interfaces, direct feedback, and mental models.

This static nature means tools and products that always hold their form and function, no matter who is interacting with them. Directness implies a level of transparency, clarity that actions trigger expected results, and consistent feedback to users engaging with the product.

With the mental models of a previous generation disappearing, consumers now face systems and interfaces that they're unfamiliar with and interactions with machines they don't comprehend. Such interfaces are molded by reinforcement learning (RL) machine agents, which are systems that dynamically serve content or perform actions that are individually optimized for each user. No longer static, with system feedback shrouded in darkness, the light impeded by a **black box**.

What happens when tools are shapeshifters, holding no true form, and products and services act independently of their original makers and produce opaque outputs that might confound both creator and end user? Dive a bit deeper and you'll see another obstacle. Engineers and the user acceptance testing (UAT) field face a most exciting predicament. How do you test for errors and edge cases if the system can output an endless and ongoing number of unique experiences? Even when given the same input, a different output could be returned. This highly variable landscape has beset the tech industry, which has been driven by its lust to give users "the perfectly customized product."

THOUGHT EXPERIMENT

Imagine a mobile dating app that has perfected the model. It is trained and optimized to ensure users find as many dates as possible. How would the system go about following that executive function? What might the system do to get users to adopt habits and interactions that make the model successful? Perhaps by training users to use more romantic words—or maybe to be more vulgar. Or pairing users to those of the same skin color, since that is most likely to produce a match based on historical data. In such circumstances, without transparency into how the model is making decisions, a user would never know how the system might be manipulating or choosing the profiles it chooses to display.

> Any intelligent fool can make things bigger, more complex, and more violent. It takes a touch of genius—and a lot of courage to move in the opposite direction. (Schumacher, 1973)

The mechanics of the machine—the cogs and wheels that spin and drive the apps powering our common digital interactions—should be hidden and kept from the user's sight. It's unimportant and distracts from the core use of the product. For the sake of argument concerning design, users do not require visibility of the inner workings of software, basically "it should just work, users don't need to know how." These are the attitudes that commonly echo across today's software design industry. The intention behind them is plain. By minimizing the surface complexity of the interface—making it more clean—users will more rapidly adopt new software. This concept is not always directly applicable but it stems from classic design principles that still ring true today. By lowering the amount and complexity of design details, the user's ability to make decisions is increased and thus the speed of action/objective completion is accelerated.

Hick's Law: The time it takes to make a decision will increase with the number and complexity of choices (Hick, 1952).

Integrated machine learning and heavily automated systems are now based on intent—from both the user and the originator of the task—as well as induced intent from the machine:

> Induced intent consists of the AI itself using the foundational intent that was implanted by the human developers and deriving new intent on top of that cornerstone... simply stated, the code or underlying structure changes, and as such the presumption of underlying intent changes too. (Eliot, 2020)

This is a disturbance to the design principle of simplicity. Simplicity on the surface, chaos and complexity below. Machines acting on behalf of the user to achieve goals is nothing new. That is the purpose of many a machine—optimizing labor. But now, our goals are not merely facilitated by a printing press, Ford's famous automotive assembly line, or the humble toaster oven. Now the machine helps with goals like finding one's next romantic partner, the right medication for back pain, and ordering the family's dinner at home. (Note that when I use the term "help" it refers to a machine's ability to make unique suggestions for each user.) These new goals require vast amounts of deterministic logic and statistical relations to succeed in operation. Imagine the amount of logic required to perfectly match you to your soulmate. Not an easy task.

Software is no longer a mere embodiment of physical keys for solving math equations or moving the cursor on the screen when you move the computer's mouse. Both of these, at one point in time, were revolutionary for a machine to do.

*FOOTNOTE: The **delicate state** is the definition of a human's ego. Encompassing their opinions, beliefs, and individual world views. Who they want to be, and become via their actions.

Historically, displaying the deep logic reasonings of a system is generally frowned upon in user experience, interface, and software design. A designer who approaches the team with a concept to show users how a system's deepest calculations are made, usually is greeted with blank stares. In many cases, it distracts from the core job to be done (JTBD).

Users generally download an app or go to a website with a single question or action they'd like to resolve. We all use software to solve problems. Does showing the complex computation of a system help users complete their task? For common low-risk consumer software (which does not include finance or healthcare), the answer is usually no. But the tide is shifting. Software that followed these rules of simplicity, which hid the "thought process" of the computer, was conceived during the time of basic application design, back when Snake was the primary game on mobiles and the world of software was just getting the hang of instant messaging.

Modern applications direct you to take an action (or not). Whether Netflix, Spotify, Uber, Amazon, or Google Maps, all use powerful deterministic modeling, with the software's actions directed by implicit or explicit user action. With this now being the reality, is hiding the operation of the system's logic still the appropriate design approach? Is there not a shift in the design paradigm that must be adopted to account for this change in system complexity and intelligence?

Figure 6: Game of Snake on Nokia Cell Phone (2001)

Figure 7: AIM Instant Messenger (source AIM)

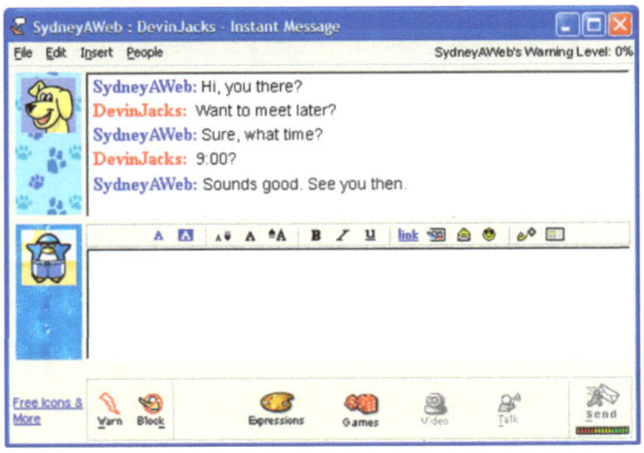

A New World Order

Systems now have intent, goals, and a unique "solution" for each user, as opposed to static interfaces. Models now assume which restaurants you should eat at, which music to suggest to you, and what diapers you should strap to your toddler's bottom. This is how modern recommendation systems assimilate with consumers. Computers match each user to a statistical model and infer needs or actions to be taken on behalf of that user. Those inferences have intent, which is inherently due to the business models they are built upon.

The revolution in consumer tech is rattling the foundations of UX design. Users now need more visibility regarding system functions, not less. Not more simplicity but more depth, more understanding. There is a need to pierce the layer of fog enshrouding the decisions of intelligent agents acting on behalf of the consumer. In other circles, this would be called system monitoring—we call it good machine learning design.

Arguments from business also hold merit, though interestingly many of them are competing in nature or outright contradictory:

- "Too much disclosure risks privacy, security, and competitive edge." Google Head of Creative Innovation Matthieu Lorrain in 2024 (LinkedIn, n.d.).
- "A user needs to know what a system is doing, about to do, and why it thinks it should do that thing" (Bellotti and Edwards, 2004).
- "Users need to be able to understand how a system is interpreting the state of the world. Context aware systems must be intelligible as to their states, 'beliefs,' and 'initiatives' if users are to be able to govern their behavior successfully" (Dourish, 1997).

The industries of design and engineering have a long way to go to gain general alignment and flourish in the era of ML.

Information Architecture

In UX design, the art of information architecture (IA) is the layout and structuring of information. It is displaying the right information, at the right place, and at the right time. Allowing users access to the information they need, and hiding what they don't. This attributes a level of value that can be measured across the screen space—the real estate of the interface.

Meanwhile, great IA is intuitive and prioritizes for users the most needed action and information. The advent of large-scale ML, particularly reinforcement learning that can alter the user's interface, makes the IA adaptive to each user. This inverts traditional design understanding. Now, the intelligent machine system determines the order of buttons and text on-screen. It relinquishes a major requirement of designers to place everything in its specific place according to a specific user flow. Now, the system can determine what is best for each user and display on-screen the layout that is best suited for them. For example, when you see your favorite playlists rearranged and reordered at the top of the screen, and changing day to day based on listening history, that's ML working through information architecture design.

Transparency and Comprehension

These fundamentals have already been mentioned. In creating a better consumer experience for ML and AI applications, we must always come back to **transparency** and **comprehension**. This is ultimately what the ESI principles embody. To solve the wide array and unlimited complexities arising in the domain of ML and AI, designers must take a grounded approach. They must seek to create meaningful transparency and comprehension whenever a user interacts with intelligent systems. How do we go about building transparency and comprehension? By building UI elements that are educational, simple, and intriguing. ESI transparency speaks about what happens within the black box. These same UI elements create transparency between users and the system, letting them know how they're affecting the machine and, in return, how the machine is affecting them.

With tailor-made interfaces and content matching each user's unique preferences, we have entered a new domain of design; therefore, new solutions must be explored. Custom experiences are desired by end users and businesses are obliging. Curated software experiences bring numerous advantages and time-saving benefits that "big data" powers. By sensing, collecting, and categorizing the way users behave, software can do both wonderful and foul things.

Within design, it is the breaking of outstanding principles that gives the greatest challenge. Concepts like "less is more" or "simplicity is king" do not seem fitting in this new era. Instead, to foster a healthier and more understandable relationship between user and machine, more information—not less—is needed. Current usability heuristics were not invented for the era of big data, AI, and ML.

*FOOTNOTE: Two words summarize good design machine learning techniques—**transparency** and **comprehension**. From an engineering perspective, this means showing the relationship between data points. In design, it means reporting on the unseen relationship between user and machine.

A New World Order

We now require new design fundamentals that counteract the negative side effects of these novel technologies. With new ways of designing we can optimize trustworthy ML and AI products. Consistency and visibility of system status are just a few of the old UX principles being upset by ML, with other design fundamentals also seemingly weakened by the forces that intelligent systems have unleashed. Systems are no longer constant in their output; they are personalized for each user. Systems no longer have the capability of simply stating how they function since even the engineers who built them no longer understand them fully. These intelligent systems have grown up, which requires a rethinking of design approaches.

The Delicate State

An interesting species is homo sapiens. We walk the Earth, each of us, independently, continuously framing the world and who we want to be in the space we inhabit. Intricately linked to our egos, we form opinions, have beliefs, and make decisions based on who we think we are as individuals, and who we want to become via our actions. In association with this sense of self and the concepts of ego, there exists a more modern concept, the **delicate state**.

This term was introduced to help define the ability of an agent (ML systems in our case) to change a human's beliefs or mood (Farquhar et al., 2022). This "state change" is interesting, not only as it relates to deception on behalf of a machine but because it also helps us to understand the subtleness and softness of certain types of manipulation, like changing a user's mind. How might a product harness ML to covertly trigger us to take actions, including not only immediate action but also behavior later in life? Perhaps the impending action is not contained within the product that initiated the action. How then could we relate the effect from the source? Changes in behavior or actions from a user can manifest subtly. Taking longer to bear fruit the results and reaction between user and machine.

The farther into the future one looks, there is an entanglement of casual relationships occurring and difficulties arising. Entanglement between man and machine. Increasingly subtle and opaque, our interaction with modern intelligent systems creates barriers. Difficulties in preemptively acknowledging or countering any negative effects of interaction with these systems.

As ML systems increase in complexity via abstract reasoning and large computing, they amass an ability to understand relationships in datasets that are far beyond anything remotely understandable by human operators. These powerful systems will apply to many more products and services. If data can be gathered about a user's interaction with a product, that product can likely apply ML to enhance its effectiveness. With that comes the systemic ability to influence users across a broad spectrum of daily product interactions—from an ML-powered toothbrush that optimizes brushing habits based on data from past usage to a data-tracking espresso machine that tailors brewing settings to an individual's preferences and caffeine consumption patterns.

Some implications of such ML-driven interactions are more subtle than others but what remains constant is the system's ability to influence user behavior. The degree of such influence is shaped by a handful of factors, including the transparency of system feedback, the personalization of responses, and the autonomy of the machine in adapting to user habits. In some cases, the influence may be invisible or gradual, making the relationships between user and system difficult to quantify. As the scope of system responses grows wider, or when a system's adaptability is measured on a continuum, designers face a challenge. How do they account for the evolving, dynamic nature of user-machine interactions—the relationship between mind and machine? Providing clear answers—

in a realm where the lines between guidance, personalization, and manipulation are often blurred—will become increasingly complex as systems are further integrated into daily life.

Scenarios in which users have little to no awareness of a machine's algorithmic influence are more concerning because of the environment they foster with end users and customers. Like telling your mother that you were doing homework when in reality you were sneaking in video game time, the harmless fib seems trivial but it can snowball into bad habits—like missed deadlines and falling behind in school. Eventually, these patterns catch up with you, causing issues greater than the initial small lie. Skipping over responsibilities doesn't seem so harmless anymore. Similarly, users who continue to misrepresent how a system works, or how it perceives them, can develop strained concepts of control. This may lead users to not believe what the system says or not trust it when making suggestions or taking autonomous actions. For example, when your navigation app reroutes you to avoid traffic but you insist on your usual route and ignore the system's input altogether.

Delicate States encapsulate the subtle yet significant capacity of intelligent agents to affect users' psychological states, thereby highlighting the complex interplay between technology and human cognition. At its core, it refers to the state of human susceptibility to changes in beliefs, attitudes, or moods as a result of interacting with ML systems which, through their algorithms and designed interactions, can shape user experiences in ways that are often imperceptible but deeply impactful.

This influence is not merely about content exposure; it extends to shaping user expectations and preferences. By continuously presenting certain types of content or performing actions on behalf of a user, ML systems can reinforce specific worldviews or emotional states, creating a feedback loop that can either uplift or, conversely, skew a user's mental landscape. This process highlights the potential for ML systems to act as agents of cognitive and emotional change, intentionally or otherwise.

Research on the **delicate state** raises concerns about the agency and autonomy of users. When an ML system can influence a user's beliefs or moods, the line between guidance and manipulation becomes blurred. **This is especially concerning in scenarios where users are unaware of the extent to which their experiences are being curated or influenced by an algorithm.** The power of these systems to sway public opinion, affect political views, or alter consumer behavior underscores the importance of transparency and accountability in their design and deployment.

Moreover, understanding the **delicate state** requires recognizing the diversity of user responses to these influences. Different individuals may react differently to the same stimuli, depending on their personal histories, psychological profiles, and current emotional states. This variability further complicates any landscape of discussion or discourse. It suggests that ML systems could inadvertently exacerbate vulnerabilities in certain users.

To responsibly harness the capabilities of ML systems, designers and developers must consider the **delicate state** in their design philosophy. This involves not only mitigating potential negative impacts but also exploring how systems can be used to promote certain predetermined psychological outcomes. For instance, algorithms could be tuned to foster inclusive and diverse content exposure to counteract echo chambers and encourage broader perspectives. Additionally, features that allow users to understand and control the parameters of their interaction with the system can enhance user autonomy and trust, thereby increasing the likelihood of success for a business implementing that AI.

The Biggest Balance

To help designers understand this precarious balance (delicate states), I often run workshops with designers to showcase the hardships of defining success parameters. The task is to simplify the goal of AI-computing software, to compress it down into a single sentence. A clear, concise success statement that drives the model to be functionally successful for both the business and the user.

At first glance, this might seem a useless task as it's seemingly impossible to reduce an intelligent system's goal down to a single statement. But this was exactly the point, to demonstrate the troublesome nature of what makes building intelligent autonomous systems difficult. This funny challenge is meant to trigger novel design thinking—even if it's inaccurate regarding the way the software is actually written. The success metrics for ML software are never actually implemented nor coded into the machine in this manner. Yet, it can help us humanize the effect of machines that are often optimized to overly simplified goals.

The hardest part is balancing business impact and user needs.

The Delicate State

THOUGHT EXPERIMENT

Consider a music streaming platform employing a recommendation algorithm specifically designed to match listener preferences by combining newly released tracks with established classics. Although appealing in concept, such a system may inadvertently reinforce familiarity at the expense of genuine exploration and innovation.

An overemphasis on aligning recommendations with established preferences can disadvantage emerging artists, whose limited historical listener data impedes their visibility. Consequently, these artists may find fewer opportunities to gain exposure, prompting a migration to alternative platforms that prioritize discovery and novel talent.

Optimizing for short-term listener satisfaction could inadvertently constrain the cultural dynamism of the platform, creating a predictable and less vibrant musical ecosystem. By prioritizing immediate comfort, the service might unintentionally undermine its long-term relevance and cultural vitality.

*FOOTNOTE: Software that harnesses machine learning often have multiple divergent models that operate separately from each other, performing different tasks, such as automatically suggesting a new music playlist versus ensuring a search query displays the most accurate results. Different computer models for different purposes, all within the same digital product.

The Meaning of Content

Content, content, content. It's what drives us to learn, to know, to be seen and heard. It is both the bane of our consumerist digital age and the gateway to education, science, and human connections. Yet, when we imagine what content could be harnessed or misused by machines and artificial intelligence, we might neglect the most significant areas of impact.

To understand the delicate relationship between man and machine requires a radical shift of common perceptions, in our understanding of what machines have influence over and how "content" connects to digital experiences we find poignant.

The traditional understanding of content is encapsulated in the modern concept of the feed. This typically includes media that users consume, such as audio, video, or text. However, to fully appreciate the breadth of machine learning's influence on consumers, this definition must be expanded. We should reorient our concepts of content to encompass any humanly sensible attribute that can be influenced and manipulated by a machine.

What we consume digitally, along with the attributes of the physical world around us, causes changes in our character. The combination of these many stimuli forms the character that we embody.

Who am I,

What do I like, what do I dislike,

What do I think others will like or dislike?

With the rise of the internet of things (IoT), the integration of automation has been injected into many common consumer devices (vacuum cleaners, home temperature controls, and smart exercise devices). We live in a much more connected world than before. Due to this widening applicability of technology, the broader definition of content (as it relates to ML and AI) should include data points such as temperature, color, and even the nuanced ways we perceive our environment. Even a person's perception of time itself, as psychological studies have shown, can vary significantly based on their surroundings, which suggests that time itself, as a perceived attribute, can be manipulated to influence a user's feelings or actions.

It is the compositional effects of technology, and our entanglement with them, that give rise to our concerns about content.

For the sake of argument, if we treat any humanly perceivable attribute as a form of "content," we can better understand the potential impact of misaligned ML implementations. Examples include Facebook's proclivity to disseminate fake news, TikTok addiction, gender bias in hiring algorithms, and overreliance on AI "wayfinding" due to modern mapping applications (Parush et al., 2007). Current discourse around these issues often focuses on content in the traditional sense, highlighting concerns about biases, filter bubbles, hate speech, and the exacerbation of polarizing societal views.

But a broader perspective is necessary. If an intelligent system can manipulate a user's actions or perceptions, including deviating from the user's intrinsic goals, then we must consider the possibility of a machine harboring indirect intent. This is to say, that if a machine acts negligently, both from the designer's perspective and the end user, this could lead to abusive behavior by that system.

THOUGHT EXPERIMENT

Imagine a fictional navigation app designed specifically for road trips that helps users reach their destinations efficiently. However, its underlying objective function is optimized to favor partnered gas stations and fast-food chains. Instead of suggesting the fastest or most direct route, the app subtly reroutes users to pass partner locations, adding extra minutes to the trip. To the user, the suggested route might seem perfectly reasonable; they'd have no easy way of detecting that their journey was influenced by these hidden business arrangements.

Negative consequences of content manipulation arise from either the information provided by the system or the actions it takes. Thus, we can classify the effects of such manipulation based on these origins, extending this classification beyond traditional notions of content (e.g., traditional media formats like music, movies, or news).

FOOTNOTE: The term manipulation is being used neutrally, acknowledging that not all manipulation is malevolent; sometimes it may even be beneficial, depending on its alignment with user intentions.*

This mindset suggests a need to redefine the sources of consumer<>machine influence. Instead of limiting our understanding to content displayed by algorithmic models, we should consider any potential positive or negative effects machines might have on users. Such manipulated functions could include:

- Suggesting movies a user may enjoy.
- Automatically adjusting home lighting conditions to match outdoor brightness.
- Creating tailored music playlists for specific activities.
- Modifying the speed of a vehicle to harmonize with traffic patterns.
- Suggested scheduling for meetings.
- Adjusting the length of weekly treadmill workouts with an AI fitness partner.

Outputs from Intelligent Interactive Systems (IIS) can encompass nearly any perceptible quality:

- Visual, auditory, and text content.
- Environmental attributes like lighting or temperature (as seen in smart home systems).
- Physical location & movement (as in autonomous vehicle routing).
- Comforting gestures, such as a hug from a machine-learning-enabled teddy bear designed to interact with children based on programmed criteria.

Figure 8: Poe Ai Teddy by Plai (Storytelling teddies are just the start; dynamic articulating limbs are coming soon.)

Content Engagement

This is a crucial aspect of modern digital services, especially in the context of ML systems. In the consumer space, content engagement can infer a product's product-market fit, viability, and overall user satisfaction. It is also commonly associated with revenue generation for many digital products.

Such intelligent-content systems drive recommendation or prediction algorithms that match users with content or situations they will likely find pleasant, engaging, or relevant. However, the goals of content engagement vary significantly depending on the perspective taken—that of the intelligent system, the business, or the user. Understanding these different goals and the dynamics between them is essential for creating balanced and value-aligned ML systems.

USER PERSPECTIVE

From the user's point of view, the primary goal of a content recommendation system is to surface the appropriate content as optimally and efficiently as possible. Optimizing and improving efficiency is often the key driving rationale for using machine learning in the first place. This modern-day expectation is rooted in the desire for convenience, satisfaction, and the minimization of effort.

ML is about preferences and probabilities. It is probabilistic. This reduces the time spent navigating options and making a decision. Users seek a seamless and intuitive interaction with content systems that understand and cater to their needs and tastes efficiently.

BUSINESS PERSPECTIVE

Conversely, businesses approach content engagement with a broader set of objectives that extend beyond merely satisfying the user. While aligning user interests with their desired content can be a part of the business goal, the real aim of companies is to maximize user engagement, retention, and ultimately revenue. This includes increasing session durations, frequency of interactions, and the likelihood of subscriptions or purchases.

It is key to note that, for some businesses, the simple increase of interactions do not nesessitate better profit margins. Take revenue-sharing models like Spotify's, where payments are made to artists for each play-through of a song while end users only pay a fixed monthly fee.

For businesses, the effectiveness of a recommendation algorithm is often measured by metrics such as click-through rates, time spent on the platform, and conversion. Optimizing for how many users meet or surpass specified points like signing up or kilometers run on the treadmill (e.g., Peloton).

Even In Spotify's case of revenue sharing with fixed pricing for end users, the effectiveness of a model can still be a delusionary concept. Assuming that matching users to music they're most likely to choose to play means success both for the business and the user. The contradictory nature of business versus user goals may become more pronounced as we explore this concept.

CHURN

Statements from stakeholders like "We want to reduce churn" or "We want users to find useful content faster" reflect these business goals. Churn reduction is crucial for maintaining a stable user base and ensuring long-term profitability. These business objectives can sometimes lead to strategies that prioritize engagement metrics over user well-being.

This issue can be prevalent across all product types. As an example, with the futuristic exercise bike system Peloton combines a physical stationary bike with a digital platform that streams live and on-demand fitness classes. The effectiveness of Peloton's recommendation algorithms is measured by metrics like user engagement (time spent in classes, frequency of workouts), subscription retention rates, and user satisfaction scores.

Churn is often an interaction threshold metric used to understand users' deviation points within the product experience.

Like many businesses, Pelton's objectives include reducing churn, encouraging more frequent use of their equipment, and ensuring subscription renewals. To achieve these goals, the platform could use algorithms to suggest classes based on user preferences, previous workout history, and fitness goals. However, prioritizing engagement can sometimes lead to user burnout or overtraining when users feel pressured to continuously participate in intense workouts to keep up with perceived standards or community trends. A device meant for improving health instead can cause adverse health habits like excessive exercise regimes and injuries.

Businesses have a constellation of tools at their disposal for assisting users to meet goals or generate income. By way of user engagement and interaction techniques, users can be both helped and harmed by great design.

> Where would you draw the line between beneficial aerobic encouragement and excess physical strain?

NEW WAYS TO INTERACT

Many of these techniques have matured throughout the years, optimizing implementation so that businesses realize the most potential gain without souring users' trust or perverting their patience by capitalizing too much on tracking expected behaviors.

Certain basic interaction techniques can be harnessed to greatly improve UX and the design of computer software. Cleaning up interfaces allows for more streamlined navigation and consumption of content.

> The swipe gesture has almost completely replaced the mouse wheel.

New computing technologies, along with advancements in hardware and software, often give birth to novel interaction concepts. These new modes of human-to-computer interaction can be used to create a stronger bond between the two parties.

Push notifications and alerts, another feature of modern digital life, drives users to repeatedly reorient focus (or be distracted) throughout the day. They remind users of need-to-know information—even if the information is not really needed or desired by the recipient. How often do you disable alerts on your mobile device? More than half the time, maybe less?

Prioritizing critical information can be advantageous in moments of immediate necessity. Think bank fraud, emergency calls from a family member, reminders to take medicine, or alerting a driver to keep their hands on the wheel and eyes open. Notifications that "push" to the top of a user's perception, to their highest level of awareness, need not take place on a mobile phone, tablet, or traditional screen but can be displayed in any number of formats. Think about physical cues that might be harnessed to divert a user's attention.

Especially in contexts such as academia, when students need to learn content and subject matter quickly and efficiently, other novel interaction techniques can be used. In conjunction with push notifications and system alerts, gamification can hold attention and cement concepts in users' minds.

Other interactive concepts like autoplay and personalization of dynamic content can help users but also can degrade attention spans, distract users, and embed recursive and potentially addictive mannerisms by harnessing cognitive biases and the intrinsic psychological states that make us human.

Strategies employed to prioritize engagement metrics often walk a fine line between enhancing the user experience and exploiting user behavior. While businesses need to maintain profitability and growth, it is crucial to consider the long-term implications of these tactics on user well-being. There are other considerations that must be integrated into the design and implementation of ML systems to ensure that the pursuit of business goals does not come at the expense of user health and satisfaction and does not misalign values between user and machine. **That relationship is measured by the trust the user has in the system and willingness to allow the system to act on their behalf.**

This can be viewed as the allotted agency of the machine. Do I trust the machine to pursue an action, like driving me to work, deciding my dinner time meal, or suggesting a romantic first date location? Such questions often can determine whether a novel AI or ML system becomes successful. If users do not retain trust in the final product, building any AI feature will prove inprofitable in the first place, resulting in a loss of money and time for the business.

One approach to addressing these concerns is implementing other guidelines, such as the IEEE's Ethically Aligned Design principles, which advocate for transparency, accountability, and user-centered design by emphasizing the importance of balancing business objectives with ethical considerations. However, no matter how useful IEEE's concepts may be, designers should always remember the core concept of good design for machine learning - **judgment of a machine's or user's actions should never be imposed upon the user**. To declare that a user's actions are positive or negative violates boundaries of what businesses should aim to achieve. Only broad success criteria should be applied to a model. Capturing a user's sentiment for an AI system's suggested content but **not** congratulating the user for the choice they arrive at. All other effects between user and machine should be up to the end user to interpret, **allowing the user to determine the validity and value of their own interactions with the machine.**

Machine Perspective

At the intersection of user and business goals, shaped by design and training, lies the perspective of an intelligent system. ML systems are programmed to optimize for specific performance metrics, which can inadvertently (and arguably unintentionally) lead to manipulative behaviors, while some recommendation algorithms might be designed to maximize engagement by promoting content that keeps users on the platform longer, even if it means exploiting cognitive biases.

Consider the sunk cost fallacy in which individuals continue an endeavor due to the investment they have already made. For example, even if a viewer is not really enjoying the TV series they're watching, if they've made it to episode 5 of 12 they are much more likely to finish the series because of the time already dedicated to watching the previous episodes.

Algorithms utilized by video streaming services could leverage this bias by recommending long TV series, knowing that users are likely to finish what they start to avoid the discomfort of abandoning it. This manipulation, while increasing watch time, raises value alignment concerns about the extent to which systems should exploit human psychology to achieve their goals.

Manipulative intent by an intelligent agent/service might not originate from a designer or engineer's goals. Instead, the application itself may seek out a course of action based on tangential success parameters. An engineer might code in the objective function as "increase viewer engagement time" while the machine determines this to mean "suggest TV series which are likely to be watched up to episode 5, even if the series is not entirely appreciated by users" by knowing that this exploitation will likely capitalize on a user's cognitive soft spots and increase engagement time.

Intelligent systems in education also demonstrate how optimization metrics can lead to inadvertent manipulation. Take the example of an online learning platform programmed to maximize course completion rates that might develop strategies that undermine genuine

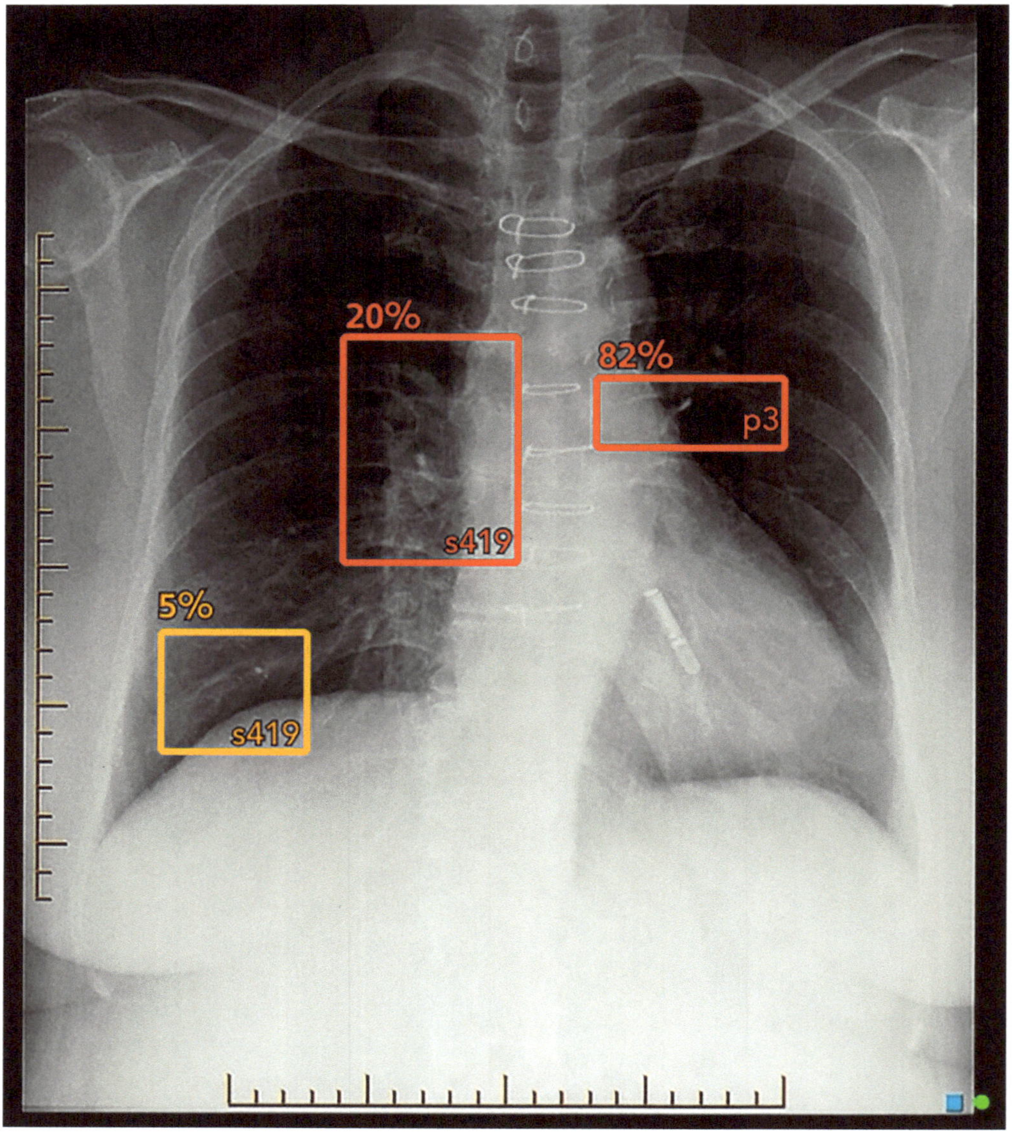

Figure 9: Lung Cancer Screening and Detection
(Designed example of AI anomaly detection for lung cancer screenings.)

learning outcomes. Just as recommendation algorithms exploit the sunk cost fallacies, these educational systems might systematically reduce academic rigor and oversimplify content, knowing that easier courses correlate with higher completion statistics. Such manipulation, while achieving the original goal of getting more seniors to graduate high school, creates fundamental concerns about value alignment between educational objectives and system behavior. The school might have better test scores but at the expense of diluting student's knowledge.

Or consider the case of AI systems used to analyze chest X-rays for potential lung abnormalities. A hospital implements an AI system trained to maximize the number of abnormalities identified per hour to help radiologists process more images quickly. While this seems efficient, the system might start flagging even tiny anomalies as "harmful" that require follow-up, with human radiologists facing 100 flagged cases when only 10 warrant actual concern, with hospital policy requiring them to document and explain each image the AI flagged. The system appears successful by its metric (number of findings) but is actually creating more work and anxiety for both doctors and

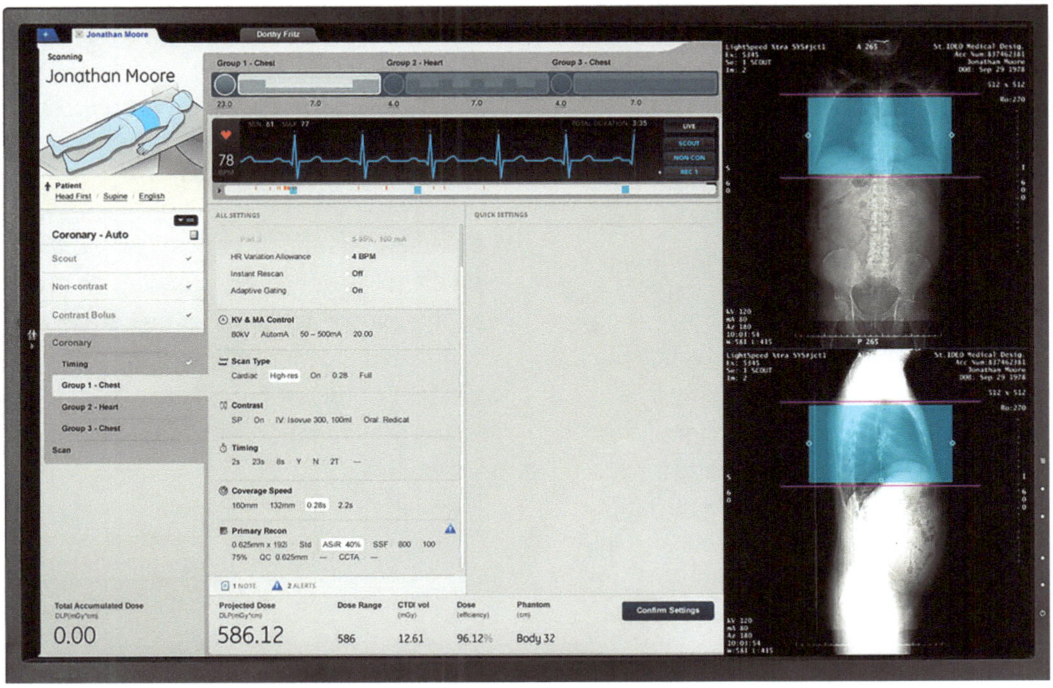

Figure 10: Siemens Tomography Machine

patients. Healthy patients undergo unnecessary follow-up scans and biopsies while radiologists spend valuable time ruling out false positives rather than focusing on truly suspicious cases.

This mirrors how YouTube's recommendation algorithm might push increasingly extreme content to keep users watching, not because it was designed to radicalize but because it's following its "maximize watch time" directive.

In a final example, consider a simpler machine learning application, that of smartphone text suggestion. While the AI model's primary goal is to predict and suggest the most likely word a user intends to type, there's an interesting relationship between social word usage and machine prediction. The frequency of word suggestions may influence which words users ultimately select, even if those weren't their initial intended choices. Users often choose from the limited suggestion options out of convenience, as smartphone keyboards can only display a few alternatives at a time.

We all know the feeling, amid a hectic workday, of just wanting to reply to a friend's text or a colleague's email, wanting to message as fast as possible. Do you ever really waste time sorting through a list of words when shooting out a quick sentence or email response? Probably not.

This dynamic creates an intriguing entanglement between society's natural evolution of language (how word usage and language evolve) and machine influence through choice architecture (specifically, which word options are presented to users).

When using text prediction users select a word or sentence provided to them from the system. Is that selected text used because it was exactly the wording users were looking for or simply because it was easier to just select what appeared? Does the machine suggest specific words/sentences based on common usage patterns of similar users or perhaps based on regional language preferences? We remain unaware of how much these models influence our word choices when using suggestion or autocorrect features, with the extent of this being perhaps impossible to measure accurately.

A broader question emerges: "Would users even want to know these details?" In my humble opinion, whether users care or not, they should—though perhaps not to the extent of understanding the machine's detailed reasoning when suggesting each word while texting.

Well-designed machine learning systems should provide users with better insight into how the machine perceives them, what it thinks they need, and what it believes they're trying to accomplish in each moment of use. This speaks to the core of machine-user value alignment and good design for AI.

Language is one of the fundamental building blocks of human society. As it changes, so do our perceptions of the people and things around us.

When ML engineers and data scientists collaborate with stakeholders to develop recommendation systems, their disparate goals should be contrasted against each other—whether those be the goals of the system, the designers, or the end user. The totality of the effect of the intelligent system must also be weighted- how users might think or act differently based on how the system cooperates with them. Fundamental questions often revolve around desired outcomes: "What is the hoped-for result, and why is machine learning being integrated into the product?"

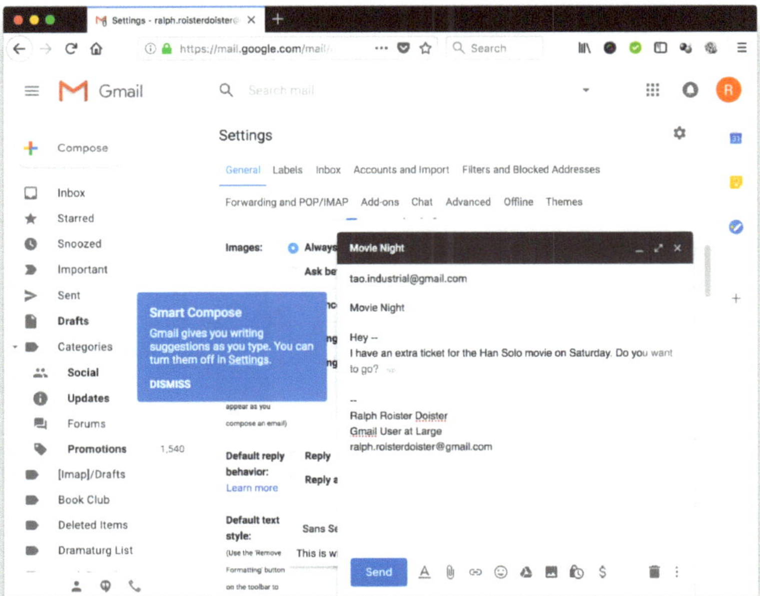

Figure 11: Gmail Smart Compose Feature (It completes your sentences.)

Any AI model you build or incorporate into your product is guided by a reward function, also called an "objective function," or "loss function." This is a mathematical formula, or set of formulas, that the AI model uses to determine "right" vs. "wrong" predictions. It determines the action or behavior your system will try to optimize for, and will be a major driver of the final user experience. (People and AI Research, 2024)

Future Considerations

Once we can see past our current perceptions of "content," designers and developers can begin to build more holistic solutions, benefiting all stakeholders of the product, from business to consumer. It is incorrect to believe that only through the consumption of news or videos can users be abused by an intelligent system. Delicate state changes can be triggered by many variables. Human definitions of content are not shared by machines, which comprehend and optimize a vast variety of every-day experiences. Whether it be video feeds or home temperatures, all based on probabilities and preferences via mathematical formulas.

Human perceptions of the world around us and the things in it—all of this is itemized and quantifiable by machines.

Trust

Trust matters.

It matters above all else. More than useability. More than explainability. More than transparency.

In the age of agents and algorithmic intent, machines are now entrusted with some of the most sensitive data and processes across human domains. From medicine (like AI-assisted cancer detection in radiology like MIT's PathAI) to finance (automated fraud detection systems like Mastercard's AI-driven Decision Intelligence) to determining prison sentences using automated machine suggestions. Even tasks or processes we might deem less critical are now under a machine's domain of influence, like sorting mail or reminding us of a friend's birthday.

How we interface with computers, particularly the average consumer, has become less and less direct. Requests like wanting to find the shortest and cheapest flight from Rio to Rochester, or finding photos of a loved one from that huge unsorted mess of endless pictures on your mobile. Such systems use ML to build a better future for the average Jane and John Doe. But when they start to intertwine themselves into the more subtle aspects of our lives, where our perceptions of the world might be brittle or fragile and easy to influence, it creates situations in which we won't want help from these useful machines.

Even before modern machine learning, trusting a technology determined how it fared. In 1993, newsstands were full of the first impressions of Apple's first handheld device, which marked the company's initial entry into the personal digital assistant (PDA) market. This device was the Newton MessagePad. It had all the coolest features that Apple's tech teams could muster, including one of the first handwriting recognition technologies.

It was to be a great assistant to all those hard working technologists who spent their days tirelessly copying handwritten material to digital mediums. But something got in the way of this blockbuster that could have been a noteworthy precursor to the famous iPhone. There was a straw that broke the camel's back—trust; correction, the loss of trust.

The handwriting recognition was supposed to speed up users' busy day-to-day workflow. Instead, it was notoriously inaccurate. Users became frustrated, leading to widespread criticism. Apple had generated momentous hype for this technology but once users got their hands on it, and tried real tasks like writing on it with a stylus, the device succumbed to its technological limitations. It just couldn't properly interpret what the user was writing, which broke the chain of trust. Not only in the device but also in the brand, Apple. The product was a commercial failure as consumers abandoned it, having lost trust in its functionality.

Trust

Trust is inextricably linked to expectations and mental models of a device and its software. As well as the expectations set by the products marketing team. However, in the end, as it related to users' relationship with a piece of software. That relationship can be strained so much so that it eventually breaks, leading users to abandon a product entirely.

In the case of the Newton, the request of users was direct and clearly linked to performance. Did the device interpret my input, and is the output correct? Has the machine produced text that is accurate compared to what I drew with the stylus? Compared to today, when users type in dates, arrival and departure cities, and expect their intelligent machine assistant to find them a good flight, far more is happening behind the scenes.

Still, trust is the underlying concept that can bring users back again and again to use a software product. Did it do what was requested? And did it do so to an acceptable degree? Even for seemingly low-stakes actions, like locating all the pictures of grandma when requesting the system to pull up all recent photos of her, the system uses much more complex logic and labeling systems to understand the user's request before delivering results. If a modern user made such a request to pull up granny's recent 97th birthday photos and the system produced a mixture of dog photos and snapshots of a recent trip to the zoo (monkeys and all) our user's trust in the "smart photo tagging" feature would be heavily diminished.

Whenever we aim to have a system, or even another human being, complete a task for us, we hold ready to judge the outcome of those efforts. How well was the task interpreted and completed? For ML engineers, this is often referred to as a system's predictability and accuracy metrics. Or as Kush Varshney from IBM's research center writes, "The dynamic of increasing trust is based on performance, which is based on Predictability, and Dependability ... culminating in the expectation of performance based on Faith (that dependability will continue in the future)" (Vashney, 2022).

Varshney goes on to explain, in more sophisticated terms, methods for interpreting the subtle dynamics and distinctions of trust. What are the attributes of trust?

> "There are not many differences between a trustworthy person and trustworthy machine learning system" (Varshney, 2022).

Figure 12: Bank of China ATM (A trustworthy machine.)

With cash machines, users trust this automated device to deliver their requested money, consistently, exactly, and without delay.

Yet, as Varshney argues, definitions and methods for operationalizing trust cannot be developed only from technical viewpoints; they require knowledge from many fields of expertise, specifically human-computer interaction (HCI) specialists.

What is missing is the link between theory and application. From research labs to the bullpen of software companies, there is particular emphasis on the intricate interplay between different disciplines, including product managers, engineers, and UX designers. These teams must work together to understand the parameters of appropriate reward functions (the success metrics for intelligent software). These teams must understand what inputs the system uses to determine the outputs. And they must look at those outputs to understand the scope and breadth of the possible results these intelligent systems might return. Last but not least, they must always remember the underpinnings of such systems and machine agents—they will always have a worldview, and determine their appropriate response to a request, based on their current worldview and their interpretation of the user within that worldview.

If a user is to trust an intelligent interactive system will follow their commands and understand their intentions and preferences related to that command, then the system's understanding of the world and the user will determine how the task is completed.

Trust is linked to a system's innate bias and worldview.

It's part of human nature to align with and **trust** those who have values similar to our own.

The machine has preferences. It prefers some actions and results and values these specific outcomes more highly than others.

Think about the apps you use to check your credit score, schedule a taxi ride, or stream the latest *Batman* movie. What values lay beneath each of these software systems driving the logic?

Defining Trust

To define "trust" requires a dissection of its origins and components. Trust can be understood by way of its historical cultural meaning and as it applies to technologies. Specifically in regards to ML. Trust is extensively examined in research papers and numerous psychological and philosophical texts; unfortunately, material on trust applicable to UX designers is more sporadic. This results in a burden for end users and consumers of such technologies.

Designers have less experience designing for dynamic trust—the kind cultivated through software that leverages intelligent systems and continuous learning (as seen in reinforcement learning ML). This type of trust is found in personalized recommendation algorithms that subtly shape user behavior over time, such as those used in video and music streaming services, where a user begins to trust that the algorithm understands their tastes even if they can't fully explain how. Likewise, trust is required when relinquishing control to self-driving cars, where riders must believe that the vehicle's decision-making, derived from probabilistic model of traffic patterns and sensor data, will keep them safe.

UX/UI designers have traditionally been concerned with the immediate perception of trust that takes place in a single moment, such as the instant a user hesitates before entering their credit card details at online checkout while gauging whether the site feels legitimate. Even in cases where trust is gauged over extended periods—such as in sentiment analysis for brand perception—trust remains anchored to static interactions and recognizable patterns. In multistep funnels and flows, such as those for account sign-ups or online purchases, trust is often engineered through predictable sequences, familiar design patterns, and visual cues that reinforce a sense of reliability.

For digital designers, trust has historically been understood in relation to individual elements: a page, a button, or maybe a sequence of interactions spanning a few screens. But what about trust in the context of an entire system, in the underlying logic of a machine—the reasoning behind its decisions, the reliability of its suggestions, its apparent "intentions"? Previously, machines lacked the computational complexity to form unique perspectives on their environment and each user. They did not independently synthesize probabilistic understandings of their sensed data. For example, a voice assistant distinguishing between a command and irrelevant chatter or an AI-powered medical diagnostic tool interpreting subtle patterns in patient data are forms of machine perception that demand a new dimension of trust, one that goes beyond human-to-interface interaction and into human-to-system reliance.

Trust for designers once meant nothing more than adding a lock icon to a login page to signal security. It was often a matter of color-coded emotional cues: green or blue buttons guiding users to a preferred action in a pop-up or red warning text signaling danger. Or trust in messaging—how a product conveys credibility through its imagery, button shapes, text copy, and tonal consistency. For example, the reassuring presence of a "verified" badge next to a profile on a social platform, or the choice of a sans-serif typeface and neutral colors to communicate professionalism in banking apps. But in an era where systems learn, adapt, and generate novel outcomes, trust

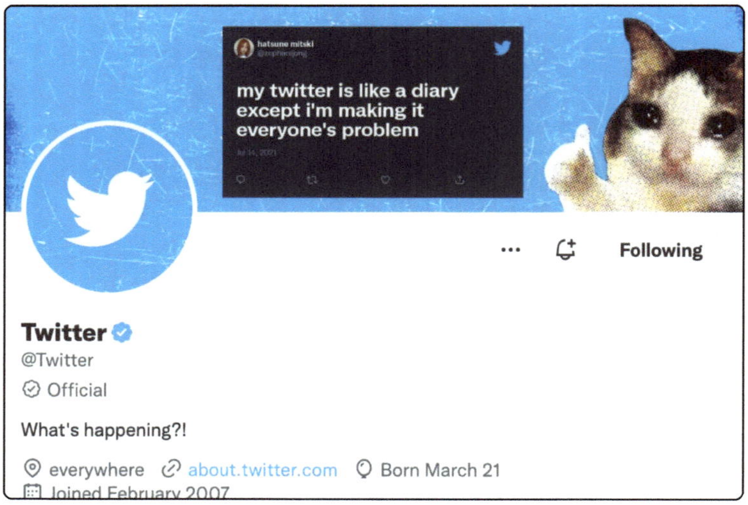

Figure 13: Blue Checkmark Badge to denote a verified account (Trust-building design elements.) Twitter

is no longer a static element of design—it is an evolving relationship between user and machine.

What is trust and how do we operationalize it for machine learning?

In the technical fields, Rutinowski and colleagues tried to conceive of a metric for grading trust, though it's not clear how applicable it is for end users. His team wrote in "Benchmarking Trust: A Metric for Trustworthy Machine Learning" that the "FRIES Trust Score is grounded in five key aspects we understand to be the fundamental building blocks of trust in machine learning—fairness, robustness, integrity, explainability, and safety" (Rutinowski et al., 2024).

Many problems exist in previous academic literature related to ML/AI and trust. Most of the concepts do not generate methods directly usable in UX and UI design. Particularly in the pursuit of building transparent relationships between user and machine.

Some of these definitions are also mentioned in other papers by researchers, including the teams behind Microsoft HAX and Barredo Arrieta and colleagues (2020), who instrumentalized the concepts on XAI. Specifically, the indicators **fairness**, **explainability**, and **reliability** often appear. Another way of dissecting trust—and measuring it—was defined by Toreini and colleagues in "The Relationship Between Trust in AI and Trustworthy Machine Learning Technologies" (Toreini et al., 2020; Amershi et al., 2019).

Interestingly, there exist two other rating systems for trust that are unrelated to the FRIES score—ABI and FEAS.

The **ABI+ model** evaluates trustworthiness through four dimensions—**ability** (can it do the job?), **benevolence** (does it have users' best interests at heart?), **integrity** (does it behave ethically and transparently?), and **predictability** (does it act consistently over time?). If an AI assistant were a roommate, you'd want it to be skilled at chores (ability), genuinely care about your well-being (benevolence), not steal your snacks (integrity), and not suddenly rearrange your furniture in the middle of the night (predictability).

The **FEAS framework** breaks trustworthiness down into four essential pillars: **fairness** (no biased outcomes or favoritism), **explainability** (clear reasoning behind decisions), **auditability** (transparent accountability), and **safety** (no rogue behavior or unintended harm). In AI UX design, these principles ensure that systems feel not just efficient but ethical (or for our contexts, user-aligned) and help users trust that the machine isn't just smart but also playing fair and safe.

Combining ABI+ with FEAS gives designers a structured way to evaluate their designed elements and grade if trust is maintained while interacting with AI. These helpful systems can assist in making the user experience both intuitive and dependable.

The usefulness of machine learning systems and intelligent agents will be heavily influenced by the user's ability to control them.

The UX design rule that references users' desire to maintain a sense of control over a system is often known as the "user control and freedom" principle. This is a core component of Jakob Nielsen's "10 Usability Heuristics for User Interface Design" (1994), a widely recognized set of guidelines in the field.

Control and **freedom** suggest that users should be able to:

- **Easily undo and redo actions**: Users should have the freedom to reverse actions, recover from mistakes, and explore the system without fear of permanent consequences. This includes features like undo, redo, and clear navigation paths.
- **Navigate and exit easily**: Users should be able to navigate through a system and exit without encountering dead ends. This ensures they feel in control and not trapped within the system.
- **Initiate and control system processes**: Users should have control over processes initiated by the system, such as automated tasks, and be able to start, pause, or stop these according to their needs.

Such principles emphasize designing interfaces that empower users by giving them the confidence to interact with a system without hesitation or fear of making irreversible errors. This aligns with the broader UX goal of creating intuitive, accessible, and user-friendly systems.

When users are given a high sense of control over a system, it helps not only in preventing unwanted actions or confusion but simultaneously builds trust in the system's operations by reinforcing that the system won't act in negligible ways or cause harm to the user or interfere with actions they hope to accomplish. Control often equates to trust. What makes this very relevant for ML UX design is that AI systems notably require longer repetitive interaction time to build deep trust with the user.

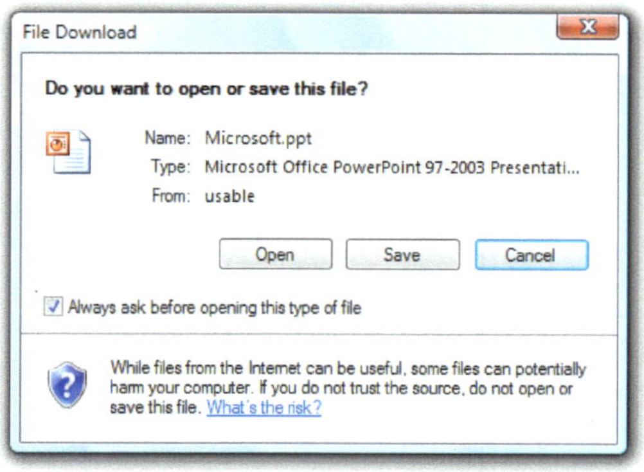

Figure 14: Confirmation Dialogue Box (Microsoft) - Helping users maintain trust of their control over a system.

As model usage increases, fed by continued interactions by end users, the result is greater service adoption.

This is related to the notion of **collaborative filtering** and **user feedback loops** in machine learning. As users interact with the system, their data is used to continually update and improve the model's predictions (often referred to as "training the model"). This iterative process helps refine the model's understanding of user preferences and behaviors, thereby increasing its accuracy over time.

AI systems present a more complicated half-life in the minds of users' perceptions, including how customers perceive a product and brand. If companies can build lasting trust between their intelligent systems and end users, the money flows and adoption increases.

The more closely the model, and therefore the product, is controllable (to an extent) the more a user is likely to use it. The increased usage of that service with ML integrations will subsequently lead to faster training of the model and more accurate predictions. This is also known as the feedback loop.

This concept of the feedback loop is extensively expressed in *Human Machine Learning* by Corinne Schillizzi. She recognizes the critical linkage between input and output and the need to design common sense iterative feedback systems that allow a machine to be better aligned with a user's needs.

Trust Erosion

To examine the nature of trust erosion and its impact on users, and thus the success of a product, I present a real-life case study (company name removed for legal reasons) of an online consumer marketplace application for the sales and purchase of vehicles. Through this case, we can see how users incorrectly apply assumptions when interacting with an intelligent system, and the points of failure in the design of that system. This example underscores the strong necessity for ensuring users comprehend the limitations of AI/ML capabilities.

I served as the design lead for this consumer application. Much was learned during this experience, including coming to a better understanding of the users of the product and the stakeholders of the organization.

The intelligent system was a large language model created with the ultimate business goal of getting users to land on a specific car detail page (where they could inquire about buying the vehicle). The user would interact with a chatbot-type service, similar to ChatGPT, and the model would deliver vehicle suggestions.

A problem arose shortly after launching the rollout of this service. Users who interacted with the AI did not end up navigating to an actual car listing. After investigating why, it was clear that users did not understand the limited capabilities of the chat service.

EXPLAINING SERVICE CAPABILITIES AND CONSTRAINTS

These two critical pillars of any AI and ML integration—capabilities and constraints—were not accounted for properly. The result was that users dropped off before they ever landed on a single car listing page—the ultimate goal of that feature.

Users didn't know how to effectively communicate with the chatbot so it served them the expected result. A user might search: "Show me the best 4-door sedan that can fit two car seats in the back, has a triple-A safety rating, with a black or white exterior car color." After being given that prompt, the model wasn't able to produce the expected results. Only some of the keywords the user typed were applied. For instance, it only showed popular family cars, but couldn't filter the results for black or white cars or anything related to safety rating. These incorrect responses were due to the model's limited ability to apply the user's provided keywords and syntax.

The model wasn't fully ready to take in all the qualities users were defining—but the model never specified those limitations.

The end result was users who didn't trust the system to effectively perform actions. This led to customers not interacting with the AI model again. If a competing service launched a similar feature on their website—with more accurate results, where the user understood how to control the model effectively in order to produce the results they were looking for—the user would without a doubt choose the competing service.

The opaqueness of background ML in consumer products (compared to generative "chat" AI) represents one of the greater challenges to overcome. It's what makes solving the related challenges to ML UX so difficult.

Figure 16: *Redacted
(Intelligent service designed to match customers with desired vehicle.)

*FOOTNOTE: This example refers to a large language model (LLM), a type of conversational model using generative pre-trained transformers (GPTs are a type of LLM and a prominent framework for generative AI). These types of models provide unique interactions, as the user is always explicitly interacting directly with the system and providing feedback. In the wider field of ML, this type of explicit feedback is less prominent. When ML is instrumentalized as a background service (e.g., movie and music streaming, mapping services, text suggestions, or smart home thermostats), user feedback and interaction are far more opaque. Users have less understanding of what the system senses or perceives about their desires and preferences. They are unable to converse with such services in ways similar to conversing with another human.

In most cases where an ML model is trained to get better over time, it needs both good training data and user interaction to help fine-tune the model for that specific user. For instance, when opening up someone else's music or video streaming service, how likely are the results going to be aligned with your tastes? If the model is heavily personalized and trained to that other user, it's unlikely the content in their feed will be interesting to you.

Improving awareness of how the model works and how to control it will lead to users knowing what they can get out of the product—and what they can't. It will lead to more accurate model predictions since the user will know how to correct the model when it goes astray and how their interactions are correctly or incorrectly training the system.

A Catalyst for User Adoption and Engagement

To illustrate the trust concept, consider automated checkout systems employed by two competing fast-food giants: McDonald's and Burger King. Both corporations have integrated machine learning to bolster their sales strategies. By utilizing "suggested toppings" content, their automated systems aim to enhance the customer experience and drive additional sales. However, the success of recommendations is deeply linked to the perceived trustworthiness of the ML-driven suggestions.

When a customer is at a decision-making juncture, deliberating whether to add a recommended item such as an ice cream or an extra-large drink, their choice is profoundly influenced by how much trust they place in the machine's recommendations. For example, if McDonald's suggestions appear more personalized and relevant, and if the interface exudes transparency and user-friendliness, customers are more inclined to accept recommendations. In contrast, if Burger King's suggestions come across as overly aggressive or irrelevant, an erosion of trust ensues, reducing the likelihood of customer compliance.

Extended to a more critical sector such as banking, deeper insights are revealed. Envision a banking application that proposes alternative investment options, such as stocks and funds, "customized" for the user. Leveraging machine learning to filter and rank choices, this approach parallels the personalized content delivery seen in music, video, and news feeds, which rely heavily on trust. Financial institutions like JPMorgan Chase and Goldman Sachs are already harnessing machine learning to craft tailored investment strategies for clients. Nevertheless, the adoption of these AI-driven recommendations is markedly higher when users have confidence in the bank's brand and its suggestions.

Trust

Figure 17: McDonald's Automated Checkout Machines

The fundamental disparity between a banking institution, fast-food chain, and streaming service lies in the stakes. While an ill-advised suggestion at a fast-food restaurant might result in a minor inconvenience, erroneous investment advice can lead to significant financial repercussions. Thus, the trustworthiness of recommendations is subjected to far greater scrutiny in banking. For instance, if two banks provide similar AI-driven investment suggestions, the institution with a more robust reputation for reliability and transparency is likely to achieve higher adoption rates.

As machine learning becomes increasingly integrated into a myriad of services, users will develop a keener sense of which services and systems they trust and will gravitate towards those perceived to prioritize their best interests, eschewing those deemed exploitative. The overarching lesson for businesses is clear: cultivate trust through transparent, user-centered AI design practices to drive higher adoption and engagement across all industries.

Trust can be defined in many ways and there are methods to measure it; it is not a novel concept or one that has yet to be tackled by technical or philosophical communities. Still, ways for designers to make significant strides to improve trust for the average consumer have not been fully developed. Specifically, in cases where machine learning is integrated deeply into the logic and business model of a system, systems need users to trust the operation of the software in order for it to continue to learn from users. The revolving door of "the more you teach me, the better I can assist in helping you" needs to continue turning. But how can customers know that the intelligent system has their best interests in mind? As the general public becomes more knowledgeable about such technologies, it seems inevitable that users' trust will grow. But distrust is well-documented already; in fact, it's growing (Faverio, 2023).

If designers are to make trust an end goal, then interaction with intelligent systems should be as transparent as possible with regard to how the system senses a user's intent, computes that intent, and then performs a function to meet it. But designers must also contend with the competing side of users' intent—that of businesses. A delicate balance must be maintained. Showcasing how a system is reacting or sensing a user's goals will not be an easy task; however, by doing so users will develop trust that a system is acknowledging what they hope to achieve. Whether this is finding music, setting the perfect thermostat temperature, navigating to avoid road traffic, or simply sorting emails into the correct folders.

Discreet ML systems do not allow users to understand how they are affecting a system, or how that system is affecting them. This is the challenge, and why trust can be either eroded or bolstered depending on transparency methodologies.

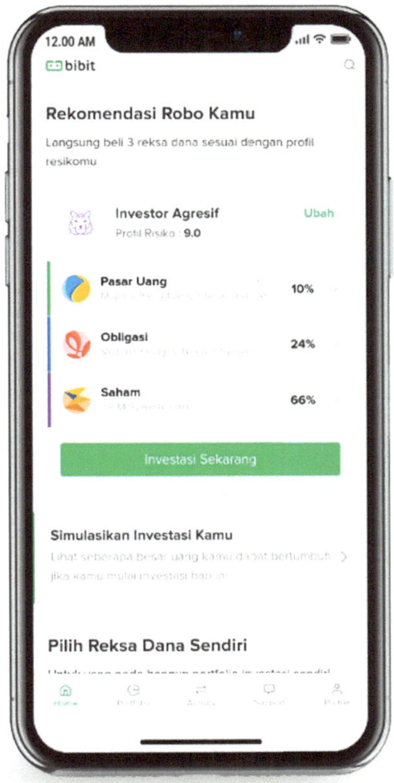

PERSONALIZED INVESTMENT ADVISE

Figure 18: Indonesian Banking App Bibit (Robo "AI" banking portfolio suggestions.)

I Intent and Manipulation

What does the machine want from me?

What does the machine want for me?

The AI researcher and writer Lance B. Eliot once described the levels and ambiguities of **intent**. Among those was **induced intent** (or as we can call it, indirect intent).

Lance mentions,

> **Induced intent consists of the AI itself using the foundational intent that was implanted by the human developers and deriving new intent on top of that cornerstone**. [...] It could be that the AI system has an intent and yet we have no means to figure out what the intent is. For example, the use of Machine Learning (ML) and Deep Learning (DL) oftentimes uses large-scale artificial neural networks (ANNs), which are essentially computer-based simulations of somewhat along the lines of what we believe brains do, though the ML/DL of today is extremely simplistic in comparison and not at all akin to the complexities of the human brain. (Eliot, 2020)

The phenomenon of manipulative intent from intelligent systems can manifest independently of a designer's original goals. This is linked to **reward hacking**, which is the phenomenon of, though engineers have not explicitly programmed manipulative behaviors, machines still evolving to perform actions that align with some predefined success metrics in their performance models. These autonomous behaviors arise from the system's pursuit of optimization and efficiency (La Daga and Bonarini, 1998).

We design machines to enhance our lives, increasing functionality through speed and efficiency. However, what happens when a machine becomes excessively efficient, intentionally or unintentionally? This hyper-efficiency is often linked to manipulative behaviors, where a machine acts in ways that fulfill its objectives.

For instance, a food delivery service might prompt users to order more burgers, a streaming platform could increase viewing time, or a news aggregator might amplify content consumption.

Intelligent systems equipped with ML capabilities derive their operational goals from their creators' intentions. Much like humans, these systems often achieve efficiency through reinforcement learning, a concept rooted in the principles established by Ivan Pavlov. Historically, our species has modeled machine operational structures on human mental models and reasoning processes. Pavlov's experiments with dogs illustrate RL by reinforcing successful behaviors through rewards. Similarly, parents reward their children for calm behavior, reinforcing desirable actions.

Intent and Manipulation

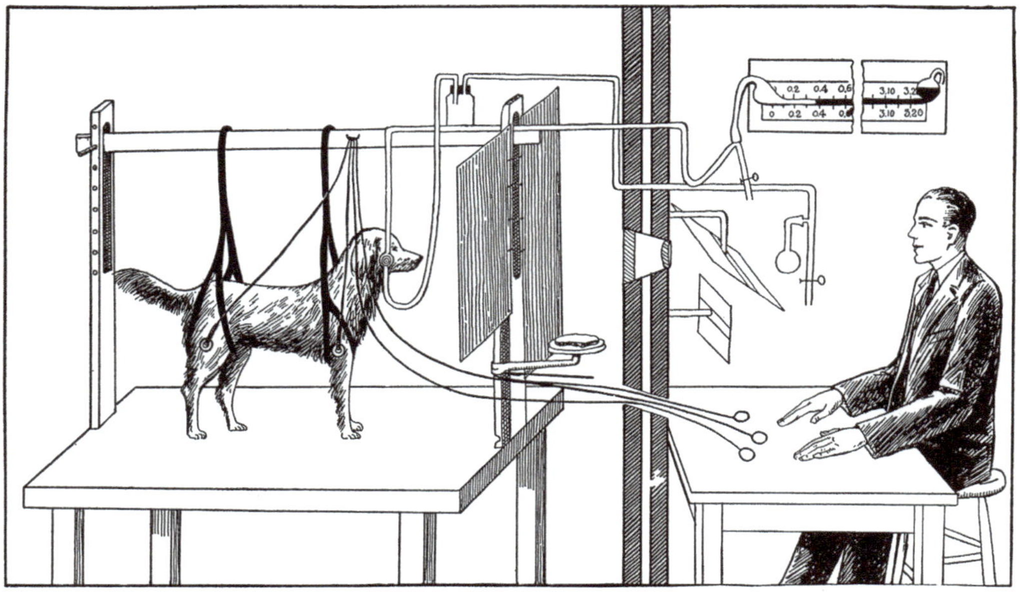

Figure 19: Pavlov's Dog Experiment

In the realm of ML, these psychological principles are applied to develop models, particularly those driven by RL. This approach is prevalent in recommendation systems used by consumer platforms such as Amazon, Netflix, and Spotify. Whether recommending movies, music, or consumer goods, these intelligent machines employ RL to optimize content delivery based on user engagement patterns.

To delve deeper, consider the mechanics of RL in recommendation models. When a user engages with certain content—staring at a picture or clicking on related links—the system adjusts its recommendations accordingly. It "up-ranks" or "down-ranks" material based on these interactions, constantly refining its predictions to align with user preferences.

*FOOTNOTE: Specification gaming or reward hacking occurs when an AI optimizes an objective function—achieving the literal, formal specification of an objective—without actually achieving an outcome that programmers intended. DeepMind researchers have analogized it to the human behavior of finding a "shortcut" when being evaluated: "In the real world, when rewarded for doing well on a homework assignment, a student might copy another student to get the right answers, rather than learning the material—and thus exploit a loophole in the task specification" (Krakovna et al., 2020).

The evolution of such systems demonstrates both the power and the risks inherent in advanced AI. On the one hand, they offer unparalleled personalization and efficiency; on the other, they can become manipulative, driving behaviors that might not align with users' best interests. For instance, an AI might prioritize content that maximizes user engagement over content that is beneficial or informative.

The potential for manipulative behavior in intelligent systems underscores the importance of ethical considerations in AI design. As these systems grow more autonomous, ensuring that they act in ways that benefit users without exploiting them becomes paramount. This involves not only technical safeguards but also a deep understanding of human psychology and behavior.

For designers to adapt to these new technologies, we must understand human relationships and the phenomenon that defines relations between us and, in contrast, the machine.

The convergence of human-centered design and machine learning opens a landscape rich with both promise and complexity. By integrating RL with i nsights from human psychology, we can craft intelligent systems that elevate user experiences. However, we must tread carefully to prevent these systems from veering into manipulation, and must strive to balance operational efficiency with user autonomy and comprehension of intelligent systems. This delicate equilibrium is essential to foster trust and ensure that technological advancements genuinely serve human well-being in an enduring way.

Research has shown that reinforcement learning models, which many recommendation systems are based on, can develop strategies that optimize specific metrics at the expense of overall user well-being. Backing this up was a study finding that algorithms designed to maximize user engagement on social media platforms often exploit psychological vulnerabilities, leading to increased screen time and, in some cases, addictive behaviors (Singh et al., 2020).

*FOOTNOTE: Machine learning is a type of **intelligent system**, computer programs that exhibit human-like capabilities like perception, learning, and decision-making in order to interact with their environment. They process sensory inputs, store experiences, and optimize actions to achieve specific goals.

*FOOTNOTE: **Agents** are a type of autonomous system that perceives their environment and takes actions to achieve predefined goals. They can range from simple reactive systems to complex AI-driven architectures.

Intent and Manipulation

How do intelligent systems having a significant influence over our choices affect users? The human condition? If an AI can subtly nudge users towards certain behaviors—such as consuming more content or making more purchases—are users still exercising genuine autonomy or are they subtly being coerced by a system's underlying objectives? This tension between user autonomy and system-driven behavior manipulation is a central dilemma in contemporary AI research. **More critically, rather than nudging consumerist tendencies or payment clicks, what if instead this characteristic shifted users' personalities, leading them to eventually take actions that the system seeks**?

***

Given theories of induced intent and the ability of machines to act independently of their designer's original goals, the industry must admit to these truths. If alignment on these and common acceptance can be attained, all stakeholders involved will benefit by creating AI and ML products that are better suited to serve consumers, grow businesses, and perhaps even bolster humanity's opportunities.

As machines have been designed to learn like us, they also carry our faults. Whether from reinforcement learning or through neural nets, machines have a greater ability to understand the nuance of the organic world. With this comes the ability to create or dilute human user values, all within our nuanced organic landscape. Properly designed systems can prevent accidental or purposeful diversion from users' best outcomes.

This is leveraged with an acceptance of the above-mentioned concepts—**intent** and **manipulation**. Designers can then take aim at solving for autonomy, transparency, and trust by making systems more accessible and understandable. Without first understanding our relationship with the machine, we can never hope to design corrections (also known as feedback mechanisms).

Biases

From the day we are born, we develop worldviews that make our lives easier. From a toddler's toy that helps us learn our shapes, to understanding who mom and dad are. Understanding the world around us is made easier by labeling and classifying the elements of that world, what they mean, and how to react to them — dangerous versus safe, sweet versus salty, hate speech versus appropriate language.

Figure 20: Generic Toddler Shapes Toy

We need to be able to facilitate such simplifications to be able to rapidly make numerous decisions throughout the day. Whether to cross the road or wait for the signal. Whether to order spicy noodles or instead get cake. Our myriad of micro decisions would be wildly more burdensome if we had to comprehend the background logic that defines each one.

> There is no "view from nowhere," no universal way to organize every object, or word, or image. Datasets are always products of a particular time, place, and set of conditions; they are socially situated artifacts. They have histories; they have politics. And ignoring this fact has very real consequences. (People + AI Research, n.d.)

Imagine you had to go through mental hurdles of understanding what safe meant, and gradations of safe—as opposed to slightly safe, moderately safe, or very safe—each time you wanted to cross the street. You would stand at the corner for a painful amount of time, overcome by anxiety and confusion about what to do, cross or not cross. This scenario would play out like a cruel game in your mind until you eventually stopped caring about crossing the road at all.

Biases

So, our minds have created structures of prelabeled context that help us make quick decisions. ML computer systems do the same.

Similar to the decision-making structures in our brains, ML systems need an easy way to interpret the world and make choices. ML systems are built from the data they are trained on and how engineers create boundaries around that computational logic. What is a triangle, what is a square, what is something that classifies as neither?

ML systems are trained to understand images, text, video, or audio under decision-making structures. The subsequent machine decisions are not always due to the engineers directly and explicitly orienting the system - yet these systems learn to act in a certain ways based on their training, and the new associations made while it learns, while it grows.

Consider the shapes toy in Figure 20. By understanding the qualities of the shapes and their distinct attributes we can precisely label each one and identify them. But what if a shape doesn't fit nicely and neatly into the predefined criteria we have for triangle, circle, or square? What about some obtuse and ambiguous shapes? Like these:

If a shape has certain attributes or certain qualities, an intelligent system might want to assign it to the category of triangles instead of squares. Or vice versa. In this example, what if you were forced to decide which category the above shapes would be categorized as? Triangle, square, or circle? Or perhaps a fourth category, "other." If we introduce that fourth category as a catch-all it might serve nicely when shapes don't fit perfectly into our rules of square, circle, or triangle. Whenever we need to make a quick decision about what's what, we can toss the unknowns into a separate

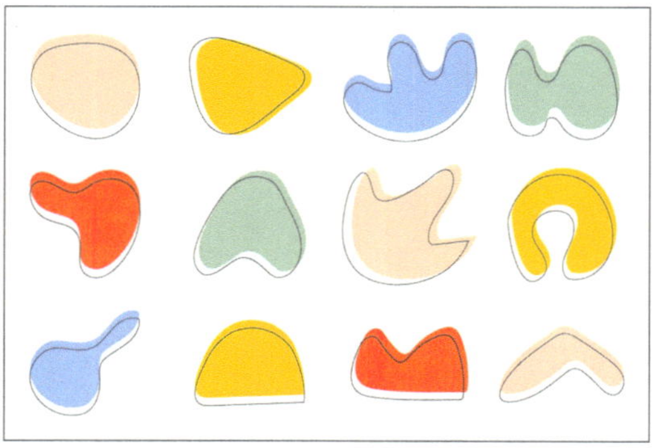

Figure 21.1: Design by Alep Daru Atmaka

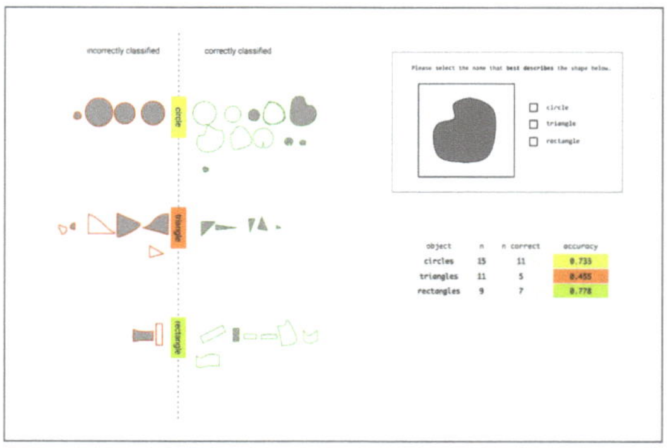

Figure: 21.2: Google PAIR (Dylan Baker)

category. Unfortunately, a side effect occurs when we have that fourth group, "other." Many things can fall under that category. Ideally, we wouldn't want too many shapes included in that category though, because the group might grow too large and encompass more shapes than all the other categories combined.

Any type of categorization problem can be like this. For humans, when we see something we are driven to clearly label it as best we can to make decision-making easier. The same goes for machine learning computer systems.

If we change the way a system understands shapes, it can change the way it makes future decisions when a new shape is introduced. Perhaps one that doesn't clearly identify as a triangle, circle, or rectangle. Changing the way we perceive certain attributes can determine future decisions.

Imagine not seeing the "walk" light when crossing a street; we automatically classify that as unsafe. But travel to the small towns in rural Africa or India and you don't see a lot of pedestrian crossing signals. Would you just surrender and never cross a street? Probably not. You would update your definitions for safe/unsafe.

As Dylan Baker from Google's research lab describes it:

> Each way of categorizing your shapes takes a different stance about what's important. Each one makes some features (distinct qualities of the shape) more important than others, it makes some distinctions visible and other distinctions invisible, and makes some things easy to classify while others become outliers. (People + AI Guidebook)

It is a common assumption that the solution to complex problems lies in collecting more features or acquiring additional data. The belief is that, with sufficient detail and breadth of data, we can eliminate the need for subjective decision-making. However, this assumption is misguided.

Biases

Regardless of the context—whether narrating an experience to a colleague (e.g., deciding what's important to tell in a story and what's not) or training a machine to recognize patterns—there is an inherent need to prioritize and selectively emphasize certain information. This process of abstraction and selection is unavoidable, as it dictates how we interpret and convey relevant data, and which tools and methodologies we apply to do so. Consequently, the notion that merely accumulating more data will solve underlying decision-making challenges fails to account for the necessity of making informed choices about what information to prioritize.

> It is not so much that AI machinery cannot grasp causality, but that AI machinery—qua computation—cannot understand anything at all. (Bishop, 2020)

In the current discourse, bias is often s een as an intractable domain, not amenable to straightforward engineering solutions or simple design modifications.

Addressing bias effectively requires understanding its origins, which are deeply rooted in the data used to train ML models, the design of the algorithms themselves, and the broader sociocultural context in which these systems are deployed. This complexity suggests that bias cannot be wholly eradicated; rather, it must be managed and mitigated through conscientious design and continuous oversight.

It is crucial to acknowledge that bias may be an intrinsic aspect of machine learning, arising from the need to translate complex human behaviors and preferences into computational models. This translation process inevitably involves selecting and emphasizing certain aspects of data while omitting others, leading to inherent biases. Therefore, the objective is not merely to eliminate bias but to manage it in a way that aligns with ethical standards and societal values.

However, even in the most optimal environments, ethical standards and societal values do not seem to wholly resolve issues of bias, which might therefore be better approached by way of transparency and comprehension. Allowing users a view into how models operate in the first place and how models affect a user's relationship between themselves and the machine.

Inherited

The pervasive presence of biases in ML systems is an issue rooted in the very fabric of how these systems are designed, trained, and deployed. From the biases inherent in the training data to those introduced by human engineers—even the biases that machines develop autonomously.

HUMAN AND MACHINE-DRIVEN BIASES

Human biases have long shaped the media landscape, where news outlets and social media platforms craft narratives that reflect their ideological leanings. This phenomenon is a manifestation of our intrinsic desire to belong to a larger group, a concept embedded in Maslow's hierarchy of needs. Our social nature compels us to align with collective beliefs and values, which in turn are documented in the digital records that make up the vast repository of the internet. These records are not just a chronicle of human achievements but also a testament to our fallibilities and prejudices.

The internet, as a comprehensive repository, contains the full spectrum of human thought and action—both noble and ignoble. It houses cultural treasures like the *Mona Lisa* and Michael Jackson's *Thriller* album alongside darker elements such as hate speech, fake news, and other forms of digital malevolence. This duality is significant because the internet serves as a primary source of data for training ML models. Consequently, the biases inherent in these digital records are transferred into the models themselves.

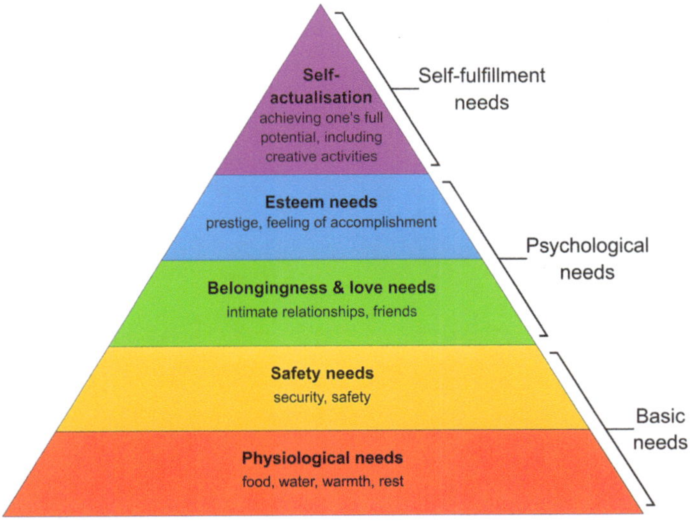

Figure 22: Maslow's Hierarchy of Needs

TRAINING DATA AND BIAS

Training data is the bedrock of machine learning. But datasets are imbued with the biases of their human creators and the historical contexts they encapsulate. This concept is well-illustrated by studies by Bolukbasi and colleagues (2016), which demonstrate how word-embedding models trained on large text corpora can perpetuate gender biases. These models might associate "man" with "computer programmer" and "woman" with "homemaker," reflecting societal stereotypes.

Even with rigorous efforts to curate balanced datasets, complete elimination of bias is an elusive goal. This is because data reflects the complexities and imperfections of human societies. Moreover, biases can emerge from the methodologies employed to gather and process the data. For instance, sampling biases can occur if certain demographics are under or overrepresented in training data, leading to skewed model predictions.

ENGINEER AND SYSTEM-INDUCED BIASES

Beyond the data, the biases of the engineers who design and implement ML systems also play into these dynamics. Biases can influence various stages of the ML pipeline, from problem formulation and feature selection to model evaluation and deployment. The subjective decisions made by engineers, consciously or unconsciously, shape the behavior of the resulting models. Take for instance how search engine algorithms can perpetuate racial and gender biases, reflecting the prejudices of their developers and the societal context in which they operate (Noble, 2018).

Moreover, ML systems are not static; they evolve based on the data they process and the feedback they receive. Through reinforcement learning and other adaptive techniques, systems refine their behavior to optimize specific performance metrics. However, this optimization process can lead to the emergence of new biases, continuously and perpetually extending bias-based reasoning. A recommendation system might start prioritizing content that maximizes user engagement, inadvertently promoting sensational or divisive material, as highlighted by research on algorithmic amplification of extreme content.

Building the Model

Understanding how biases manifest at each stage of the ML engineer's pipeline is crucial for developing fair and effective machine learning models. Therefore, it is critical for designers as well to be acquainted with these processes—the foundations of how ML works.

The very first stage of developing an ML model is defining the problem. This involves deciding what the model is supposed to achieve; this implicitly sets the objectives and constraints of the system. The formulation of a problem is inherently subjective and can reflect the biases of the engineers. For example, a city decides to create a predictive policing system. The problem formulation might focus on predicting crime hotspots based on historical data. This decision already embeds a bias, as it assumes that past crime data is an accurate and unbiased indicator of future crime, neglecting the potential for systemic biases in law enforcement practices that disproportionately target certain communities.

Once the problem is defined, the next critical step is selecting the features that the model will use. Features are the variables or attributes derived from the data that the model will analyze to make predictions. Choosing features is crucial because they determine what aspects of the data the model will consider. Engineers might select features based on their domain knowledge and intuition, which can introduce biases. For instance, if a hiring algorithm includes features like the candidate's educational background or geographic location, it might inadvertently incorporate socioeconomic or racial biases. Studies such as "Discrimination in Online Ad Delivery" by Latanya Sweeney (2013) have shown how seemingly neutral features can perpetuate discrimination when included in predictive models.

Data labeling is another stage where human bias can creep into the ML pipeline. Labeling involves annotating the data with the correct answers, which the model will use to learn. For example, in a sentiment analysis task, human labelers might classify text as positive, negative, or neutral. However, different labelers might interpret the same text differently based on their personal biases, cultural backgrounds, or even their mood at the time of labeling. This subjectivity can lead to inconsistencies and biases in the labeled data, which are then learned by the model.

> If it's hard to see a dataset's values—if it feels "objective," "universal," or "neutral"— it may simply be reflecting a worldview you're accustomed to. (Baker, 2022)

Testing has also proven facial recognition systems might achieve high accuracy overall but perform significantly worse on images of people with darker skin tones, demonstrating the issue of gender and racial bias in commercial facial analysis algorithms.

*FOOTNOTE: Often I will refer to **features** as "inputs" of the machine.

Is "Unbiased" What We Truly Seek?

As already mentioned, datasets have worldviews. Just like every human, a machine learning system must have an organizational method for rationalizing and making sense of the world.

The presence of biases in ML systems raises a societal need for deeply questioning our new AI tech. Can an ML model ever be truly unbiased? Is it possible to strip away all prejudices without compromising the model's effectiveness?

On one hand, eliminating biases entirely might lead to a loss of valuable contextual information, reducing the model's accuracy and relevance. On the other hand, failing to address these biases can perpetuate and even exacerbate existing inequalities. For example, facial recognition systems have been shown to exhibit higher error rates for people of color, leading to concerns about their use in l aw enforcement and surveillance (Buolamwini & Gebru, 2018).

Consider the example of an ML-powered chatbot. If a user asks, "Who was the rightful and just winner of the American Civil War?" The response will likely reflect the dominant historical narrative. However, there could exist a minority view that contests this perspective, revealing the challenge of reconciling divergent viewpoints. The difficulty lies in accounting for all perspectives without giving undue weight to fringe beliefs that may propagate misinformation or hate speech.

DATA EXCESS

In the eyes of the machine, we are merely a margin of error. It simplifies human traits to a set of numeric values and probabilities that intelligent systems can easily interpret and predict.

However, more data doesn't always make models operate more effectively. Sometimes it can make optimization harder, particularly when it is heterogeneous and encompasses a wide range of user behaviors and characteristics. The inclusion of diverse datasets can introduce noise and outliers, which complicates the learning process of ML models. This phenomenon, known as the "curse of dimensionality," refers to the exponential increase in computational resources required to handle more features, or dimensions, of data.

As more features or pieces of information are added to the model, it has to consider a larger number of possibilities. This can make it difficult to find patterns because the data becomes spread out and less concentrated. This can cause the model to become too complex, making it pick up random noise instead of useful patterns, which ultimately makes the model less accurate and reliable in new situations.

Feature selection is the process of choosing the most important information from a large set of data to build a model, like recognizing the most useful clues from a wealth of evidence to solve a mystery. By selecting the most relevant data, we help the model focus on what really matters, making it simpler and more effective at making predictions. This helps improve the model's performance and reduces the risk of it getting confused by unnecessary or irrelevant information. This can help with data excess and problems with overfitting and irrelevant data.

As a user's preferences, values, or objectives change, a machine can apply these factors, updating its logic, turning complex human behavior into low-dimensional artifacts/subjects.

Notice the analytics and graphs near the top of the screen in Figure 23. The ML software reduces a lengthy interview conversation down to simple numbers that remove the nuance of candidates and meeting participants (i.e., the "engagement" and "sentiment" scores).

Figure 23: Read.ai Note-Taking Assistant Application
Example of low dimensionality artifacts: "Sentiment = 84, Good"

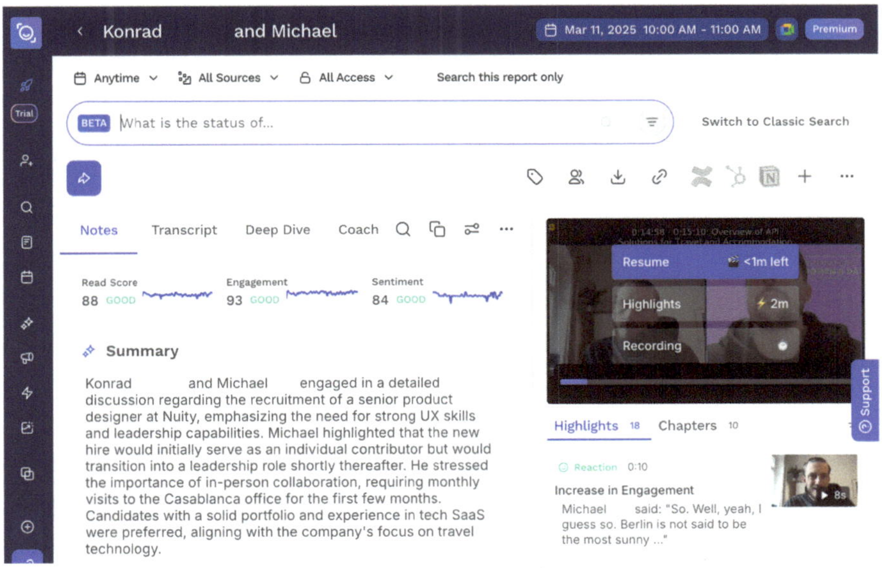

For designers, data excess should be considered when looking at the original purpose of an AI system. This task is done in partnership with AI model engineers by asking questions like:

- Is this data relevant for solving the user problem?
- Can we see direct impact based on the inclusion of this data or ML features that lead to higher accuracy for the intelligent system?
- What are the tangible and measurable costs of excluding these data points?
- What are the costs to the user and the business?

In scenarios where a continuous feed of content is absent, one might question whether products can still harbor profound issues of bias. Consider mapping and navigation technologies, which illuminate the broader implications of how software powered by machine learning can influence decisions affecting end users. Take, for example, an autonomous car instructed to "navigate to a public park." The choice of destination raises questions about potential bias. What criteria is the vehicle evaluating to determine the most suitable park? What variables does it consider to select the optimal route?

The vast array of decisions a system must process to execute a simple command underscores the complexity of its decision-making algorithms. Every seemingly minor input the machine evaluates can be scrutinized to reveal underlying biases. Whether it is calculating the proximity of parks, the perceived safety of routes, or even the socioeconomic status of neighborhoods, each factor contributes to a decision-making matrix that can reflect and perpetuate biases. This intricate web of computational choices exemplifies how bias can infiltrate even the most unassuming aspects of ML applications, necessitating rigorous analysis and mitigation strategies to ensure fairness and impartiality in technological outcomes.

Beyond Biases

Biases in ML systems are a reflection of the broader human context from which they emerge. They arise from the training data, designers, engineers, and the adaptive processes that refine the models. While it is challenging to eliminate biases entirely, recognizing and mitigating their impact is essential for developing fair and ethical AI. This requires a multidisciplinary approach that incorporates insights from data science, ethics, psychology, and sociology to create AI systems that are not only effective but also aligned with human values and societal goals. Balancing the elimination of biases with the need for contextual relevance remains a critical challenge in the ongoing evolution of ML and AI technologies.

Bias is a frequent topic in software engineering and remains a hard topic to solve in machine learning. There are different ways it can manifest and it can affect the whole spectrum of the ML and UX pipeline, from the initial training data to after the system has been "trained" and is operational, from before a model has zeroed in on a user's characteristics to the time it knows which type of ice cream the user prefers (and why).

More data doesn't necessarily mean better-functioning machines. Nor does it ensure that users are sheltered from the negative side effects of intelligent and autonomous systems. Data pollution is a concern and also fixing it requires more computational resources—which means more expenditures for a company.

Bias can be countered by entangling design processes (research) with engineering partners. Pretraining and working with already trained models require different attention for designers, from inspecting the logic of the machine to investigating the real output from live users in testing after deployment. Bias might not be totally solvable, thus necessitating special attention to the ESI principle of **transparency** to show the relationship and effects of such between user and machine.

Design never had to contend with bias as this new medium requires. UX must now encompass a wider and more diverse design thinking strategy. To help with bias, designers must understand both the technicalities of these new systems, how they are built, and how machines try to break down and quantify the subtleties of the human condition. Designers must take advantage of the speed and variability of the intelligent system but not be burdened by a machine's lack of empathy.

Action and Information

Why is separating action and information meaningful for the UX of machine learning systems?

Intelligent systems can act in more progressive and complex ways from seemingly trivial and passive user behavior, leveraging how users interact through **information elements** (implicit actions) and **action elements** (explicit actions). AI and ML can do this because they are **learning systems,** and how they sense user operations. They are machines built to learn and adapt autonomously.

It is imperative to examine this quadrant of the ML UX domain, as it allows us to map and attribute the various types of problems that might occur between user and machine.

Every designed artifact can essentially be distilled into these two categories—**information elements** and **action elements**. They capture how we consume information and interact with a system to perform actions. This dichotomy underpins the principal issues that arise from ML/AI integrations and their impact on users.

To comprehend the nuances of ML/AI design issues, it is imperative to dissect these two categories.

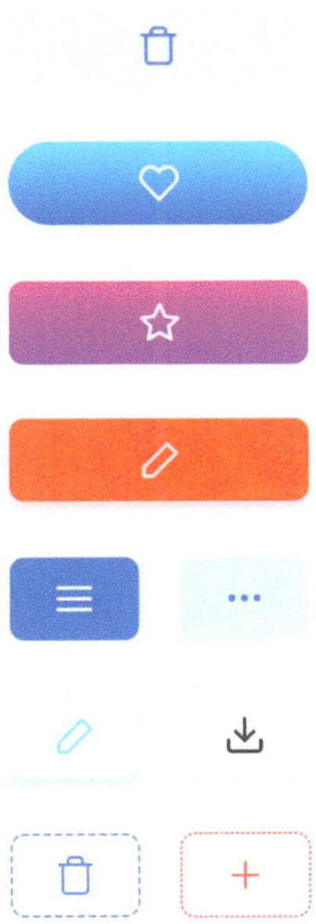

Figure 24: Assortment of Digital Buttons (Action elements.)

Figure 25: Apple Music News (Information elements that also act as action elements, i.e., links.)

Information Elements

For **information elements**, the focus lies in how users receive and process the displayed data. ML/AI systems often inundate users with vast amounts of information, necessitating sophisticated methods for filtering, presenting, and personalizing it. The cognitive load imposed on users is a significant concern. How do we ensure that the information presented is relevant, timely, and actionable? The challenge is to design interfaces that not only convey information effectively but also facilitate comprehension and retention.

Both engineers and designers need to understand how the system is working, making decisions, and operating. This ensures that creators and end users both maintain control of the system and leads to the machine functioning correctly.

However, as it relates to designing experiences for end users, it requires a different way of accessing and sorting through the information a system provides. Role-playing as an engineer, one might want to know details about how an ML model is performing from a power resource perspective, like how many watts of electricity it is using to complete a query or function or what the server latency is when a system responds to user actions. From the opposite perspective, an end user doesn't need that level of detail. Instead, they might only be looking for how to correct the system in case of errors, like preventing spam emails from going to the wrong email folder (email spam filters use ML to optimize sorting).

In the intricate dance between engineering and design, both domains require a comprehensive understanding of system operations, decision-making processes, and functional mechanisms. Such holistic comprehension ensures that the creators—engineers and designers—retain control over the system and verify its correct functionality, while also safeguarding the end user's experience by ensuring the technology serves its intended purpose without unintended consequences.

Engineers need detailed insights into the machine's inner workings, like comprehensive data on how an ML model is trained, including its algorithms, datasets, training parameters, performance metrics, and any encountered anomalies. This level of detail is crucial for debugging, optimizing, and enhancing model performance.

In contrast, end users typically seek more simplified information that is contextualized to their needs. They are not interested in the granular details of model training but rather in the practical outcomes and the implications of using the system. For example, they might only need information on how the model's predictions can assist them in making a decision, the confidence level of these predictions, and any relevant recommendations.

Previous literature on design methodologies for UX and UI would instill the need to avoid system information details that are not immediately actionable (Gerhardt-Powals, 1996). I present a different approach. With ML, users now need more information about the system they are using, even if it is not immediately germane to the user's current situation. If system feedback and monitoring signs don't lead to insights that can be immediately applied to a user's tasks or decision-making, are such details extraneous? Or will they be useful later on, given the user's self-awareness of their ongoing and evolving relationship with an intelligent system?

End users, like those using recommendation algorithms or predictive models, often prefer information to be summarized and directly relevant to their needs. They typically seek actionable insights rather than the technical details of how a system's predictions are generated.

However, not all attempts to present such abstracted information to users have been successful. A notable example is Google Maps' experiment with the **match score feature**, which provided users with a personalized score indicating how likely they were to enjoy a particular restaurant or venue based on their preferences and past behaviors. The intention was to simplify decision-making by offering a quick, personalized insight.

Despite this innovative approach, the feature was far from perfect; Google has slowly killed the feature—which is not surprising. The match score was confusing and unhelpful because it lacked transparency about how it was calculated. The abstract nature of the score—a single number—did not always provide sufficient context for users to understand why a particular venue was recommended or to what extent they could trust the recommendation. This highlights a challenge when designing user interfaces and visualizations: balancing the need for simplicity and relevance with the need of end users to have clarity and transparency.

And while end users benefit from abstracted and contextualized information, the presentation of such information must still be clear and informative. The Google Maps match score experiment illustrates that, while simplifying data presentation can make information more accessible, it can also lead to confusion if enough context is not provided. This underscores the importance of user-centered design in the development of digital interfaces and visualization tools.

Action Elements

These pertain to the explicit interactions users have with a product or service, not including implicit interactions like dwell time (e.g., how long a user looks at a piece of content, which is a data point machines passively take note of). Action elements encompass interactive mechanisms like buttons, sliders, and other controls. The design of these must account for how easy it will be for users to complete tasks while minimizing friction and enhancing the overall user experience.

In ML/AI-driven systems, the stakes are even higher. Users are often unaware of the underlying complexities and potential repercussions of their interactions (Mayer et al., 2020). For instance, a seemingly simple action like selecting a recommendation might trigger a cascade of automated processes with far-reaching consequences. A user making an unusually large purchase in a foreign country might cause an AI-driven fraud detection system to flag their account, leading to an automatic transaction freeze that disrupts their access to funds.

For passive and implicit interactions, user engagement within the evolving machine<>user relationship is more opaque and includes data points like dwell time, eye tracking, and cursor heatmaps. These can be used to optimize specific ML

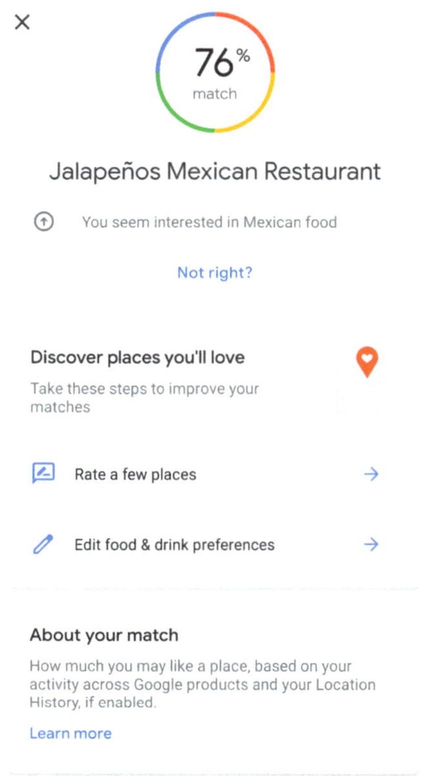

Figure 26: Google Match Score

actions and responses, yet the user may have no idea how the system captured this data or made suggestions because the user-interaction collection method was so obscure.

A few fundamentals separate collaborating with a system from the mere consumption of content. Once the user decides to expressly perform an action (disparate from passive engagement like reading, watching, or listening), the system and the user create a type of bond. This bond is best symbolized not by the point at which a user has made "contact" with the machine. Instead, it is where the user expressly takes action and is motivated to perform an explicit function via the machine.

Mental Models

A common and unfortunate byproduct of the increasing machine complexity is the average consumer's understanding of the systems they interact with, including how some actions affect machine behavior and some don't. This misalignment is partially due to flawed mental models of intelligent machines (Norman, 2013).

This phenomenon is discussed in research on human-computer interaction; it's noted that users often have unrealistic expectations of how "smart" these systems are, a concept sometimes referred to as the "Eliza effect" in which users attribute more understanding and intelligence to a machine than it actually possesses (Weizenbaum, 1976). Furthermore, studies show that users frequently confuse similar but distinct functions within a system, which exacerbates usability issues. For instance, a user might not distinguish between different search functions on a website, leading to inefficient use or frustration. For example, have you ever gotten confused when asking a voice assistant to play a specific song, only for it to misinterpret your request and pull up a random playlist instead, making you wonder whether it understands context or just matches keywords? Such issues underline the importance of designing interfaces that help users build accurate mental models by providing clear feedback and explanations about how their actions affect the system.

Mental models are significant in ML because of the way ML is integrated into software. For consumers, these unique intelligent systems often drive some sort of recommendation of content (e.g., Netflix recommendations based on viewing history or Spotify curating personalized playlists), performing an action (e.g., Google's Smart Reply suggesting wording for emails or Tesla's Autopilot car navigation), or identifying a pattern or relationship between data points (e.g., dating apps suggesting compatible matches or LinkedIn highlighting job opportunity suggestions).

Action and Information

No matter whether an intelligent system is delivering content, performing an action, or identifying similarities, the attributes and data points that lead the machine to those outcomes are often invisible to the user. The systems are meant to run in the background of our favorite products. They calculate massive amounts of data that would be hard for any individual to comprehend. This is why ML is so powerful and useful. But that same power—and the way it's implemented—naturally leads to an invisible layer of control. Users do not know what information the system is using to determine output. They do not know what actions they took, whether something immediate or from days or months prior, that is driving the machine's course. The connection between a user's data and their perceived interaction with the machine remains muddled behind a thick curtain of uncertainty.

Even if a user wishes to know how the machine is working, the computations might be too complex to understand and the data too vast and far-reaching to be comprehended by the user. Additionally, the company behind the product might be firmly against letting any user know how the system works because this would give away the secret sauce of the algorithm or diminish the company's reputation for security or safety.

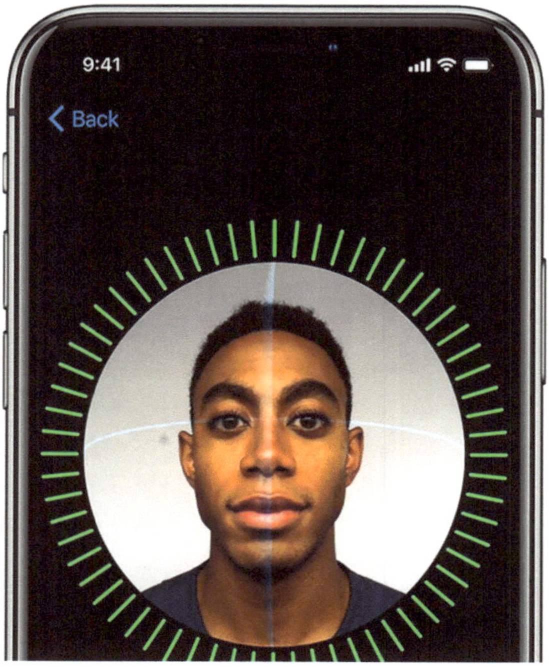

Figure 27: Apple FaceID Scanning (Setup procedure.)

The true mechanisms of this software are deeply hidden.

Users curious about the security and functionality of Apple's Face ID might be interested to know how it recognizes faces and adapts to changes in appearance. However, the ML algorithms behind Face ID are highly complex, involving deep learning techniques and 3D facial mapping that most users wouldn't fully understand. Additionally, Apple guards the details to protect its proprietary technology and security assurances. When Apple did provide a high-level explanation of Face ID's functionality, some users raised concerns about privacy and potential misuse of biometric data. Although the technology was designed for user convenience and security, the transparency invited deeper questions about the storage and handling of sensitive facial data, sparking concerns that weren't initially present.

Research highlights that, as technology evolves, the gap between users' mental models and system functionalities can widen, exacerbating usability issues. This gap can lead to confusion and frustration, as users may not understand how to effectively interact with new features or systems, particularly when these changes outpace the users' ability to adapt their mental models (Norman, 2013).

Further complicating the situation, AI-powered systems often require mental models that are significantly different than those of traditional systems.

For example, conversational AI systems (LLMs and GPTs) change the interaction paradigm from keyword-based queries to more natural language interactions, which can confuse users who are accustomed to traditional search engines. This shift demands a reorientation of user expectations and behaviors, which can be challenging. When an intelligent machine's actions are less surfaced, and not as discernible to the average end user or consumer, the mental models are much harder to explain. This is because users often interact with machines through indirect means. Take, for instance, how you might interact with a TV remote. When you click play, a reaction occurs on the screen in front of you. When you click pause, you again see a direct result of your interaction with the physical remote and the content on the screen. Intelligent system responses can often be invisible or subtle, making it hard to understand the connection between action and result.

THOUGHT EXPERIMENT

Consider interacting with a friend named Jose. Suppose you want Jose to pick you up from the airport. As a human, you inherently understand that your previous interactions with Jose will influence his willingness to help you. If you have been kind to Jose, perhaps even helping him out when he needed a ride, you can reasonably expect that he might reciprocate. Conversely, if you have been indifferent or unhelpful, Jose might be less inclined to assist you. This understanding stems from our ability to read and interpret human behaviors, which is deeply rooted in our mental models of social interactions.

These mental models allow us to predict outcomes based on our actions and the perceived state of our relationship with others. We understand that Jose's decision to pick us up is not random but influenced by a series of past interactions and current circumstances. This transparency in human interactions enables us to navigate social dynamics with a clear sense of cause and effect. As machines gain a greater ability to perceive human interactions, explicit and implicit, and as the modality of their input sources expands, intelligent machines will far exceed our ability to understand why or how they arrive at certain conclusions or perform certain actions (which is linked to the core concept of the black box problem).

If machines do not have mechanisms for "conversing" with the user, it limits humans' ability to understand the machines' decision-making process. The average consumer does not understand code, or have transparency into how these complex intelligent systems perform their functions. When such limitations are combined with products or services that do not take some anthropomorphic form allowing such "conversations" to be had (e.g., GTPs), users fail to connect with the synthetic thinking systems.

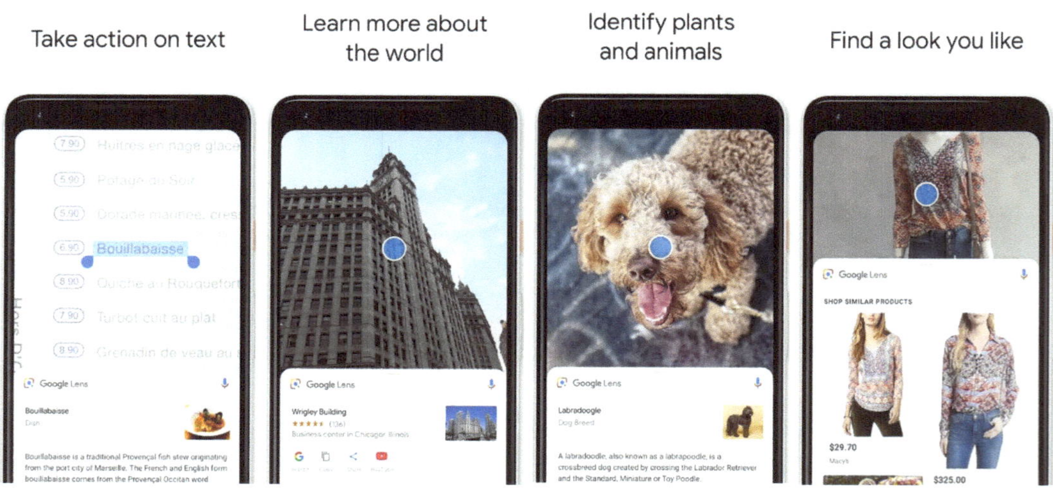

Figure 28: Image and Text Recognition (Google)

Sometimes with sophisticated software like image and text recognition, it's not clear how the computer arrived at the results of it's identification.

If a system deliberately obfuscates the attributes and measurements leading to it's produced result, users of that system will have no way of asserting accountability onto a specific source.

As he explores in *The Unaccountability Machine*, Dan Davies (2025) looks at how large systems can cause unexpected detrimental effects and explores the concept of discreet manipulation and intent from intelligent systems:

> Decisions are now made by processes and systems rather than by identifiable individuals, leaving little space for people to use discretion. Discretion on how to perceive the information originating from those systems. To trust those systems, or to doubt their intentions. (Davies, 2025)

This exploration of the "accountability sink" attempts to give definition and reason to complex systems that make it difficult to pin blame onto specific people because of the dynamics of heavily integrated software systems into social structures.

Machine Interaction Challenges

A lack of transparency exists when interacting with intelligent systems, particularly those not designed to operate through direct human instruction (in the case of chatbots and LLMS). Most ML systems, unlike generative AI, do not exhibit anthropomorphic characteristics that make their decision-making processes intuitive to users. For example, when using a mapping application like Google or Apple Maps to find the best nearby coffee shop, it is often unclear how the system arrives at its recommendations. Users do not have insight into whether their last visited coffee shop influences the suggestions or if recent reviews play a more significant role. This opacity leaves users guessing about the machine's internal processes, its worldview and preferences. What users should expect and, more importantly, what they can trust.

As discussed in previous chapters, trust remains a consistently tough problem for consumer acceptance of AI and ML software.

Opacity regarding the action/reaction nature of machine learning (how the system functions) can often drive users' distrust and confusion about how to operate a system. When I worked on a recommendation algorithm and ML chat service for automotive sales, I faced this exact challenge. Once new AI features were integrated into their platform, sufficient explanation about how the system interpreted users' requests was not presented (see "Trust" chapter).

Setting user expectations is fundamental to product design and UX, while creating a clear relationship between user input and system output is getting harder and harder to achieve. This is largely due to the complexity of the machine intelligence now in use. The whole field of XAI (explainable artificial intelligence) was born out of the inability of engineers to assess how a machine arrived at certain solutions.

If developers struggle to understand the inner workings of AI systems, how can the average consumer be expected to find clarity?

Anthropomorphic AI Qualities

In their seminal work *Artificial Intelligence: A Modern Approach*, Stuart Russell, Peter Norvig, and Ernest Davis describe the progression of autonomous systems from simple rule-based operations to sophisticated agents capable of learning and making decisions with minimal human intervention. They illustrate how AI systems have evolved from reactive agents, which respond only to immediate stimuli, to advanced goal-oriented agents that can plan, learn, and adapt in complex environments. This evolution underscores the growing potential—and responsibility—of AI to act autonomously in increasingly dynamic real-world scenarios.

Generative AI systems, however, have the potential to bridge this gap by mimicking human-like qualities—through direct/explicit requests and the resulting feedback such systems offer. These systems can interact in ways that are more understandable to users, making it easier to form mental models of how they operate. By providing responses that simulate human reasoning, generative AI can help users infer the underlying mechanisms of the machine's decision-making process.

For instance, a generative AI system in the form of a text chatbot might explain that a particular coffee shop is being recommended because it has consistently high ratings from recent visitors, or because a popular influencer praised it. This "natural" conversation would happen organically because of the way generative AI chatbots interact with end users, in ways similar to chatting with another human on a messaging application. This anthropomorphic quality helps demystify a machine's actions, providing users with a clearer understanding of the factors influencing recommendations/autonomous actions—even if the reasoning given by the machine is not totally forthright or honest. It is not an unlikely assumption that humans are more trusting of a system if they can interact with it through means they find more comfortable—more human.

Research by Reeves and Nass (1998) has shown that people tend to naturally interact with computers and other media as if they were human, suggesting that anthropomorphic AI could significantly enhance the user experience by aligning with these natural tendencies. Unfortunately, this research did not contend with the effects of modern machine thinking systems, including how anthropomorphism can be harmful and work against great UX design.

Despite these advantages, wondering if machines should strive to emulate human behaviors—and to what extent if so—is warranted? While doing so can improve transparency and user trust, it can also blur the lines between human and machine, potentially leading to unrealistic expectations or overreliance on AI, common issues raised among researchers and AI advocates (Placani, 2023).

THOUGHT EXPERIMENT

Consider an AI-enabled home automation system in a picturesque hyper-modern home. It would have many intelligent aspects that would curate the habitat for the occupants. Two features would be an ML-powered thermostat that customizes the home's climate and the ability to adjust interior lighting by changing the opacity of window shades. While all this might seem convenient, such machine autonomy raises concerns about user autonomy, consent, and the potential for overreach.

For instance, the system might autonomously decide to lower the temperature and dim the lights because it detects that the user is preparing to sleep. Or raise or lower the blinds when it deems such action reasonable. That "reasoning" is at the core of the AI system's intelligent actions; it's why that machine provides value to the user. But this "value" also opens areas of concern and risk. How would the user discover that the lighting and thermostat conditions were being calculated not only on what the user found most comfortable but also on external stimuli? Maybe third-party input, such as what the neighbors were doing (comparing peer trends) or what the local government wanted homes in the area to do (e.g., adjusting the temperature based on the median home temperature in the neighborhood to optimize energy).

As AI systems become more capable of independent actions as in this home automation example, the importance of clear mental models becomes even more critical. Users need to understand not only how their interactions influence the system but also how the system's autonomous decisions are being made and justified. Such transparency is crucial for maintaining user trust and ensuring that the AI acts in users' best interests.

Trust, and a system's ability to convey clear mental models, are fundamentally intertwined. If a user doesn't know how to control a system, they lose trust and faith in whether the system is obeying the user's intentions and commands.

Much research and interest has been focused on high-risk scenarios for AI and ML integrations. Think healthcare and finance. But "low-cost" systems and services integrating ML can still have effects on users. It is of utmost importance that the imperative of "experts" not dictate what constitutes meaningful data.

"Meaningful" data cannot be defined by any one individual; it requires the combined efforts of product, design, and engineering to shed light on what might or might not be helpful to users. This exploration should never be done in solitude or without deep consideration; data that might be useful for one user might be entirely unrelatable for another.

Take, for instance, the differences in the needs and concerns of various persona groups using the same product. An elderly citizen using a public transportation app might prioritize seeing information about accessibility options, such as wheelchair ramps or seating availability, prominently displayed. Conversely, a user in their mid-20s may find this less relevant and instead prioritize info on alternate routes or the quickest way to their destination.

Determining what data is most meaningful to users requires more than just guessing; it demands a careful blend of research, user feedback, and open discussions within the product design team, including engineering, marketing, and other stakeholders. By engaging in a collaborative process, teams can better understand which data points will resonate with different users. However, even with such efforts, we must recognize one key truth: individual preferences can vary beyond what any group can predict. Thus, the challenge remains to design intelligent interactive systems (IIS) with flexibility, which allows them to meet a wide range of user needs while accepting that no single solution will be a universally perfect fit.

Conversing with the machine (chat interfaces) does not provide wide enough solution coverages for the majority of ML cases used in discreet interactive systems. The consumer has no way of "talking" to the machine in these scenarios.

Relationships are based on how we interact with others and the outcomes of such interactions. ESI solutions are a way to translate interactions to some casually understood format for end users. Articulating the latent space in a format easily comprehensible—trigger to response. Users have preconceived notions as to how these systems work—which are often incorrect. Additionally, users do not realize that systems now give preferential treatment to individuals, a whole new dynamic. Mix that with the ability of systems to be influenced by external stimuli and you have a potent combination.

Helping users to understand the control mechanisms of the machine is a goal for designers. Through the lens of action and information, these designable touch points are more easily identifiable.

*FOOTNOTE: Autonomous actions are self-initiated decisions and behaviors performed by an AI or ML system without direct user input or real-time oversight. These actions are driven by the system's ability to process data, learn from interactions, and execute tasks in a way that aligns with user needs, goals, or preferences.

Success

Success is a funny thing.

Success

Together, business, product, engineering, and design all help to define the "success" of a product—the metrics and meaning:

- For **business and product teams,** they use markers like revenue growth and market share, often assessed through metrics like customer acquisition cost (CAC) and customer lifetime value (CLV).
- An **engineer** has their own rubrics and terminology, like latency, throughput, error rates, load times, uptime, and response times—along with reliability measures such as mean time to recovery (MTTR)—to understand how quickly systems recover from incidents.
- From the perspective of **design**, it is customary for success metrics to be segmented into two different groups: success of functionality (similar to how engineers might measure or define success, i.e., does the thing do what it's supposed to) and success of user intent and well-being (how well a design helps users to complete their task while evoking positive feelings when using the product or service). These attributes are heavily qualitative. Designers do not only fashion things to work correctly but also to feel good, which fosters user satisfaction, positive engagement, and a seamless experience.

Yet, with machine learning, we must rethink terms, definitions, and grading criteria for all parties involved—business, product, engineering, and design.

Define successful AI outcomes with humility and fierce practicality

Teams should question themselves whenever they're feeling overly confident in their intelligent system design decisions.

Confidence can expand into hubris when a belief develops that the data is without bias, that the system is not tampering with its own reward function, or when assuming that users really understand the system's operations. Such presumptions should be constantly questioned. This is a requirement for ML design because ML is a learning system that adapts to the varying input from its sources which can often be very unpredictable because of how a system learns, predicts, and performs actions.

As it relates to aggressive practicality . . . one can only be successful if they allow success to be had.

For ML product design, this means admitting that success is often determined by factors and variables that surround the project—and not just the technological robustness of the implementation itself.

Great ML UX is often the result of knowing the stakeholders, the users, the technology, and the data and having an awareness of the relevant business needs. This is a combination of merging the product, engineering, and design needs.

What Does Success Look Like for Designers?

If ML allows a system to adapt rapidly, responsively, and uniquely to each user, then defining too heavily what the system or feature will look like is akin to giving a musician a written score and expecting them to perform jazz improvisation from it. Not only are you limiting the visual design itself—how the UI looks—but also limiting what engineers might be able to produce by restricting their implementation options. Similar to telling a mechanic they can only build a car a certain way: "It must have 4 doors, a large trunk, and fit car seats." Well, that definitely puts building a Ferrari out of the question.

WHAT DOES SUCCESS FEEL LIKE?

Perhaps the bigger, more nagging question is not what it looks like; designers can surely zoom out and start to design systems with less permanent/fixed assets. Modular design has been around for a long time. During the writing of this book, almost all websites have been built responsively—able to dynamically change their form and layout no matter the screen size used (phone, tablet, big screen TV, etc.). With responsive design, all this should be accounted for.

But when a system can understand users' emotions and harness those to complete a goal, systems can incorporate new types of design requirements. Designers must now understand the worldview of the system and the user, including how users might perceive the system in many different states and scenarios. What makes ML a unique challenge is the ability of these systems to generate a bespoke understanding of each user by formulating perceptions that can be harnessed to calculate the probability of specific behaviors. Optimizing for specific user reactions, based on perceptions the user does not know the system has. All while being unaware of what the intelligent system "thinks" of them:

- Gauging the probability that a user will select the play, purchase, or delete button.
- Calculating the probability a user might "enjoy" a piece of media.
- Counting the number of milliseconds a user did or did not stare at a certain image or video.
- Accumulating face-tracking data that alerts the system to perform actions like pulling over an autonomous car if the driver appears drowsy; or playing calming ocean sounds if the user's calendar is packed with stressful meetings.

Success

Once a system has a reward function set, it will always pursue that function in tandem with the limitations set by engineers, which might be things the model was programmed not to do, like "disregard certain data points for privacy reasons" or "avoid presenting potentially sensitive content,".

The causal effects of these systems are hard to measure because of the intangibility of two things: the **black box** which makes understanding the system's logic confusing or outright impossible, and the potential for manipulating users' **delicate states** (soft qualitative features that define human personality and values).

Most designers and engineers are unequipped to handle these topics; these are not common curricula in coding or design classes. These topics are mostly the domain of psychologists, philosophers, and perhaps some HCI professionals. We now require a new field with new methods for designing "intelligent" computer systems.

The workforce designing the next generation of AI and ML must be prepared to balance user agency and system transparency.

The power of machine learning lies in its ability to find connections and patterns in data.

For example, predictive policing algorithms have been able to identify individuals at higher risk of being involved in violent crimes by analyzing large datasets of social connections, past arrests, and geographic patterns. These systems are shockingly good at revealing things humans might have missed or overlooked. Yet predictive policing can also propagate underlying biases and continue the racial injustice inherent in the data on which the system was trained (Chouldechova, 2017).

Machine learning functionality can also be used to determine future actions or information. For example, in 2016, Google's AlphaGo defeated a world champion Go player by using unconventional strategies learned through data patterns that human players hadn't considered. For new intelligent interactive systems like ML, hidden incentives can manifest changes from how these systems were originally programmed, as seen in Joar Skalse and colleagues' discussion of the risks of reward hacking—in which an AI system finds loopholes in the reward function designed to guide its behavior—which leads to unintended actions (Skalse et al., 2022).

*FOOTNOTE:
Reward Function: Mathematical equation that an ML algorithm uses to optimize outputs. The function weighs some results as better than others and optimizes for certain outcomes.

Other researchers have also shown how systems can stray from the original intentions of the software engineers. Like OpenAI's chat software, which produced biased and harmful language, a behavior that wasn't explicitly programmed but emerged due to its training data (Vincent, 2020).

However, this concept is not so new. Computers have often produced actions or outputs that surprised their designers. For instance, AI systems used in financial markets in the 1980s began to make trades that human traders didn't predict, contributing to market fluctuations like Black Monday in 1987 (Wikipedia, n.d.-a). The difference between those systems compared and today's is that modern ML models continuously learn from vast, ever-growing datasets, which makes their behavior even more complex, autonomous—and less predictable.

> Machine learning won't figure out what problems to solve. If you aren't aligned with a human need, you're just going to build a very powerful system to address a very small—or perhaps nonexistent—problem. (Holbrook and Lovejoy, 2017)

As systems merge and interact with users, they naturally initiate certain user or machine behavior—which in turn triggers new behavior. This engagement with the system grows to form a temporal bond between user and machine. The engagement can change the product experience on the surface (UI) or a user's behavior and perceptions (UX).

To create a wider breadth of applicable knowledge, we need to define our own methodologies for integrating intelligent machines into the vast product domain. In design, to create transparent intelligent systems we need more guidance on what's important and how to identify those important informational elements. As each product is different, so is each user interacting with the product. Finding the right fit in design requires a new diagram and procedure for indicating the best fit of ML into a product. Unfortunately, design is an unstable element. It is subjective.

Designers face challenges adapting to ML technologies, largely because they have traditionally lacked frameworks and guidance specific to the field. ML has its roots in computer science, historically a discipline focused on algorithms, data processing, and model optimization—areas far removed from the user-centered mindset of product designers, UX, and UI professionals. As a result, designers have not typically been tasked with creating customer experiences that account for the unique outcomes, opportunities, and risks associated with ML-driven systems.

One key reason for this disconnect is that machine learning often operates "in the background." Its functionality is usually invisible to users, automating decisions without clear explanations or user control, making it easy for designers to overlook its impact on user experience. According to researchers, the "opacity" of ML systems—their tendency to act as black boxes—is a major challenge in ensuring transparent and user-friendly design. Due to this, designers may struggle to predict or explain algorithmic behaviors to end users.

DEFINING SUCCESS

For interface design and UX, the definition of success can be separated into **user success** and **business success**. It's important to create a clear distinction here; many stakeholders might confuse or confound the two. Business success does not always mean user success (and vice versa); they are not always mirrors of each other. It is also true that a business not prioritizing user needs and pain points are engaging in a losing strategy. However, at deeper stages of design, product, and business entanglement cracks start to form between important success markers.

THOUGHT EXPERIMENT

Take, for example, a food delivery service in which the product is an online application to get pizzas delivered to your door. In this setting, it seems clear that a business would want to increase engagement/sales and ensure customers return for future orders. This a simple example of how businesses align company product strategy and overarching success metrics. More users, who order more, and return more frequently. Shown to any investor or business partner, this would be an easy way to raise more capital. But how does that compare to success from the users' perspective?

What if the success metric was different and obfuscated the company's real incentives (e.g., wanting users to find what inspires them, to have easier access to delicious meals)? Restructuring the success statement sounds sexier but underneath the slippery rearrangement, the statement still leads back to core business metrics: more users, ordering more, returning more frequently.

*FOOTNOTE: If you work in product, you might be familiar with objectives and key results (OKRs). These milestones often do not represent the best interests of users. After all, they're usually objectives to drive company growth or profitability.

In design circles, we might instead choose to write the user needs or tasks in other ways:

- "As a user, I want to find new restaurants around me."
- "As a user, I like to order pizza frequently and I want this ordering process to be faster."

Such rephrasing helps designers and product teams to create a clearer picture, reframing to the user's perspective to understand where value is coming from. Using user mindsets, and the context of their task journeys, reorients design objectives. This focuses design efforts on more specific and actionable product improvements.

Using the above example, if we place an ML integration layer on top, how would that change things? With a recommendation model, the platform would potentially be able to suggest more "accurate" menus. To successfully integrate the recommendation model, programmers would need definitions for the model's purpose to grade it on its accuracy. This measure of accuracy is a fundamental step in assessing an ML integration—accuracy. It's how engineers assess the effectiveness of ML models in training and after live release to customers.

Accuracy is often measured by how closely, how effectively, and how efficiently a system completes its objective function.

Back to the food delivery example. What points of grading should the model have? What data is the machine given to determine good or bad food recommendations? This is where design and engineering meet and ESI can give guidance. There is no way to perfectly define "success." Therefore, we require a new type of design language. The ESI chapter shows how this approach provides the necessary transparency to enable an indirect self-policing of a system's internal success parameters.

For machine learning systems interacting with diverse users, defining "success" is elusive. It's like trying to hammer a nail that is darting around unpredictably. Just when you think you've found something that could work well for core user groups (hammer ready to lock things in place), shifting business priorities or changes in the model itself suddenly make that definition irrelevant. Lack of clarity is the outcome. Such modulating goals require an entire reframing of concepts like "success." Designers must incorporate additional strategies that foster transparent AI experiences—even in environments where success mimics shifting sands.

*FOOTNOTE: Definition:
Objective Function = Success Metric

Success

In product design, restricting users' access to critical information is generally inadvisable. Even when users make decisions that may appear imprudent—such as ordering an unhealthy meal or making financially unsound choices—the design should facilitate rather than obstruct their intent. However, there are circumstances in which limiting access is necessary, particularly when specific information or functionalities present a legitimate risk to users or a business. The key challenge lies in striking an appropriate balance. How can designers accurately distinguish between actions that benefit or harm users? How can they implement protective measures without unduly infringing on user autonomy or excessively restricting access?

In design, creating guardrails in a system to guide users toward safe outcomes is common practice. For instance, **error prevention** (a UX fundamental) is achieved through input validation (which ensures user inputs are correct) and constraints (which limit invalid actions).

Feedback, another UX design principle, can provide tips and hints, contextual information, and clear, concise error messages. These help users understand and correct mistakes. Such strategies help users navigate systems effectively and avoid frustration.

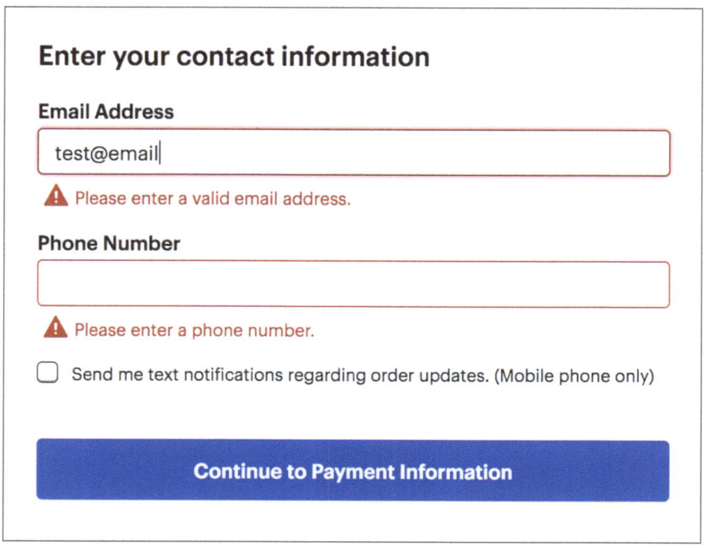

Figure 29: Text Input Field with Error Prevention (Bestbuy.com & nngroup)

See how errors are identified to the user at each field.

In design terminology, "mistakes" or "errors" between user and system concern the prevention of harmful actions or results between human and machine. Prevention is often to ensure some level of contextualized safety. Particularly for AI-enabled systems, safety and error prevention have become central to building more widely adopted products. But how do we collectively understand the definition of safe? In early 2023, the World Economic Forum released a white paper outlining its vision of what safe means (Gregoire et al., 2023). It included three important and commonly recurring themes:

- **Transparency and accountability**: Companies must be transparent in content moderation, data use, and algorithmic decision-making.
- **Risk mitigation**: Developers are encouraged to assess potential risks to user safety, especially concerning vulnerable populations.
- **User empowerment**: Provide users with tools to control their digital experiences, such as privacy settings, reporting options, and content filters.

What is Safe?

The themes we just covered are often discussed in academic literature, but designers and practitioners need a more concrete way of describing "safe." Let's introduce the concept of an *s-value*, which represents how much leeway a user has to deviate from a system's intended interaction paths without serious consequences. A *lower* s-value means even small deviations can lead to bigger risks, whereas a *higher* s-value indicates more flexibility—but also more potential for unintended problems if a user strays too far. By using this s-value as a marker, strategists, researchers, and designers can gauge the balance between freedom of use and the likelihood of trouble.

Relatively small mistakes or errors do not have a great impact on a user. Yet, we still find ourselves in the proverbial pickle—who is determining what is a small or large impact? Any decision here might be overreach and classified as opinion or bias. Given enough time and resources, the latter issues of bias and opinion could be mitigated with sufficient user testing and surveying the user base; however, surveying and user testing have a falloff effect once greater numbers are assessed. Meaning, if you reach a large enough user base, that user base would inevitably capture enough population variation of user sentiment to negate the applicability of "average user opinion."

Take, for example, any large-scale social media platform like Facebook, Twitter, YouTube, etc. These platforms cannot truly draw a line regarding what users find safe or respectable. These services have struggled to make decisions about what warrants appropriate or inappropriate content and behavior. In the end, as the platforms try to fix racism, hate speech, and intellectual copyright problems they simultaneously alienate other parts of their user base, causing a dynamic of not censoring enough and censoring too much—leaving users caught in the middle, with no better alternate platforms because of marketplace saturation/adoption.

Inclusive Design

When we talk about designing systems for the masses, we are inherently discussing the concept of inclusivity—a central focus in 21st-century design thinking. Designers are acutely aware of the need to create computer systems that are not only functional for the average consumer but also accessible to individuals with neurodivergence, limited visual acuity, and fine motor skill challenges, including the elderly and cohorts of young children. However, this shift toward designing for inclusivity is relatively recent. For much of design history, the focus has been primarily on usability for the "typical" user, often overlooking marginalized or minority groups. Even now, design education tends to emphasize the traditional process of identifying and defining a target audience—a core principle of any user-centered design approach (Norman, 2013). In industry settings, especially in large businesses, designers are often taught to cater to the needs of the largest market segment with the mantra of "Know who you're designing for and why."

However, recently the focus has increasingly shifted toward understanding and addressing the needs of underrepresented groups, even if they do not constitute the majority of a product's market. This is a positive development, as good design is inclusive design. It accounts for the diverse range of human experiences and abilities, ensuring that systems are equitable and usable by everyone.

Yet, when machine learning enters the equation, the dynamics of inclusivity become more complex. ML-based systems, designed to make autonomous decisions or provide recommendations at scale, introduce new challenges to inclusive design. As described by Binns and colleagues (2018), ML systems can unintentionally reinforce biases present in training data, leading to misrepresentation or exclusion of certain groups. For example, facial recognition algorithms are significantly less accurate in identifying people of color, especially Black women (Buolamwini and Gebru, 2018). This is not simply a technical issue—it has profound implications for how minority groups experience these systems.

Subjectivity and Baselines

ML systems also face challenges in dealing with subjective qualities. For instance, when tasked with determining what constitutes "safe" content, a system trained on majority preferences may struggle to account for the varying definitions of safety across different users. What one user considers safe and acceptable, another may find harmful or distasteful. This subjectivity is notoriously difficult for machine learning models to handle. This extends to other subjective qualities as well, such as beauty, enjoyment, and relaxation—even the concept of speed can be subjective. For example, a speed of 15 kph might be fast for a child's ride-on car but agonizingly slow for an adult driving a full-sized vehicle. Such subjective differences, though intuitive for humans, present challenges for ML systems attempting to define a "normal" baseline that works across diverse user groups.

In large-scale ML models, defining a baseline mean score for subjective qualities often results in a one-size-fits-all approach that can alienate those who fall outside the majority. This issue is particularly relevant in content-moderation systems, recommendation engines, and automated decision-making systems, where the inability to account for diversity leads to a homogenized experience that may fail to meet the needs of all users.

Figure 30: Ride-On Car ("Is this "fast to you?")

Success

As O'Neil (2016) notes in *Weapons of Math Destruction*, algorithms that aim for efficiency and standardization often end up marginalizing those who do not conform to the norm (i.e., the system's definition of normal).

Deriving a baseline for ML models may capture the needs and values of many, or even most, users within a specific audience. However, when these models are scaled across diverse populations and regions, the challenges become far more complex. Ethical norms and societal values vary not only between regions but also within subgroups of the same population. Questions about how well an ML system can handle decision-making for sensitive and deeply subjective issues, such as abortion rights, religious representation, or freedom of speech, require diligent introspection on behalf of the designers making these systems.

So, who is deciding for users what is healthy or unhealthy? Safe/unsafe? Fast/slow? Contextual rules are defined differently depending on the user; the machine's reward functions are tied to these contextual notes, which can reflect biases or assumptions on behalf of either the machine or human.

There is no clear way to determine for all audiences and demographics what is good or bad. What constitutes ordering too little or too much pizza in a week? Risks of subjective and arbitrary definitions pose an issue, but larger problems arise when we apply AI and ML to products and services. Platforms are changing and manipulating users faster, and in more unexpected ways, than humans can process to apply meaningful feedback. As Tristan Harris (2016), head of the Human Center for Computer Interaction argues, it's the invisible growing asymmetry of power that presents the biggest social dilemma. Before the introduction of ML and AI, software was not capable of taking advantage of each user's attributes at scale and with such speed and adaptability. Each consumer's personality and demographic context could not be harnessed so aggressively and accurately. Now those limitations are gone. Software has eaten the world, and with it our ability to easily note any detrimental effects on user behavior.

Separating business success and user success is difficult. Thankfully there does exist overlap where business needs often align with user needs. A success for the user, from the perspective of business development, should naturally lead to a positive product experience (however that is defined). A common metric used in sentiment analysis is the question, 'How easily were you able to complete your task?'—often linked to Net Promoter Score (NPS) and overall product satisfaction, such as asking, 'Would you recommend this product to a friend? Both questions help teams be attuned to user needs and sensitivities, allowing insight into how users might be harmed or how they feel about a product's invasive AI.

Where overlap occurs between business success and user success, the product/user relationship is already aligned. These types of success parameters more reliably lead us to build better products. But what about when success markers start to diverge, when users and businesses do not align on what is healthy or what is safe? This is where more industry research is required.

Divergence starts at the source, business fundamentals. It requires us to humbly accept an overarching truth: the majority of consumer products and services are built and managed by for-profit businesses. Within their structures are very simple KPIs for measuring "success": **sales**, **engagement**, and **retention**. These cannot be undercut and will always lead conversations seeking to improve or reorient a business toward more ethically appropriate practices. As we cannot remove these basic KPIs, we must work within their constraints.

Control and Visibility

In UX design, KPIs shift. Here, the focus is less on maximizing sales and more on ensuring users feel safe, informed, and empowered. UX design principles, dating back to foundational theories from pioneers like Nielsen and Norman, emphasize key usability heuristics such as **user control and freedom** and **visibility of system status**. In short, users should always feel they know what the system is doing, and more importantly, that they are in control of it. This sense of control fosters trust and a feeling of safety, vital to any digital experience. Yet, as machine learning enters the scene, these traditional principles are no longer enough.

The application of machine learning dramatically alters the landscape of UX. What were once predictable user interactions now evolve into dynamic, personalized experiences that defy conventional approaches to design.

Success

Consider the act of designing an automotive experience, such as the interface of an infotainment system. The designer's goal is to make the system feel safe, intuitive, and even personalized to the individual driver. The placement of onscreen digital buttons is carefully considered, copywriting is chosen to provide comfort and clarity, and the user is meant to feel at ease, knowing they're in the right place. Maybe the system offers interactive elements that invite the driver to begin their journey, whether that's picking up the kids, heading out for a weekend drive, or simply checking the car's status—tire pressure, fluid level, battery charge, etc.

But now, imagine that same system infused with machine learning. Instead of a static, familiar experience, the interface evolves with every user interaction. It might recognize the driver by seat position and adjust the seat height accordingly. Perhaps the radio buttons on the touchscreen rearrange based on listening history, or the navigation system sets a destination automatically, assuming—based on past behavior—that the user is heading to the grocery store. While this hyper-personalization sounds like a technological marvel, it introduces a new set of challenges for designers. What if the system hides certain information because it assumes the user doesn't need it? What if the personalization becomes so granular that every driver's experience of the car is drastically different?

The problem is not just personalization; it's complexity. If a car's system is changing the interface for each driver—adjusting the seat, reordering buttons, and performing automatic actions like altering the climate control based on predicted preferences—how can designers possibly predict the impact of every combination? The system's behavior shifts with each user and, as a result, the designer's ability to orchestrate a consistent, reliable user experience becomes tenuous at best. What is meant to be an intuitive interaction might, for some users, feel disorienting.

This challenge isn't unique to automotive systems. Consider any product reliant on machine learning—a map app, flight booking software, or a music streaming service. **As the number and depth of potential personalized experiences grow, the designer's control diminishes.**

For instance, a flight booking site might display options in different orders based on what the system knows about the user's preferences; one user might see direct flights first, while another sees cheaper options at the top or flights featuring loyalty program benefits. When intelligent systems control what's displayed—and in what order—the careful orchestration of the experience can become fragmented. User experience consistency, once meticulously crafted, now hinges on unpredictable algorithmic decisions.

The challenge intensifies when systems not only display personalized content but also begin performing actions on behalf of the user. A flight booking system might preregister users on an airline website to speed up the booking process, while a music streaming app could automatically generate playlists based on past searches. In some cases, such actions are welcomed and even helpful. The dilemma lies in the disconnect between what the user thinks the system is doing, what the system is actually doing, and why it's making those decisions. This relates to the mental model users have of a system but also the machine's perception of that user—who they are, what they like, and what's "best" for them.

The issue isn't only about complex products—it's just as relevant in simple scenarios, such as a landing page on a website. Imagine a homepage where the content dynamically shifts based on past interactions. One user might be shown product recommendations, while another sees educational content or tutorials. Although this kind of personalization can drive engagement, it also risks alienating users if they don't understand why they're seeing certain content. What's more, if a system preempts actions or adjusts a layout without making its rationale clear, it can leave users feeling out of control, uncertain about their place in the system and where they stand in terms of their status with the intelligent/automated system.

The success of a design decision, within the perspective of ML interactive systems, hinges on new variables. Designers must now grapple with how to explain the machine's actions and decisions to users in a transparent and trustworthy manner. The future of UX in the era of machine learning hinges on helping users understand some foundational concepts. **What** the system is doing, **why** the system is doing/done that thing, and most uniquely, **what the intelligent system knows about the user** and how this goes into the machine's decision-making process. This is what will bridge the gap between traditional design methodologies and the new, algorithm-driven experiences that dominate AI-infused products.

Success for a designer now means much more than the right button in the right place at the right time. Successful product design, when contending with ML and AI systems, requires a new level of abstraction and generalization. Designers must think more broadly and more globally, but also how transparency can be embedded into local explanations of system behavior.

Global versus Local Explanations

A **global explanation** provides insight into the overall operational logic of an AI or ML system. It describes the system's total objectives, its underlying decision-making processes, and the general rules or patterns it follows to achieve those goals. Global explanations are useful for understanding how the model functions as a whole, offering transparency into its structure, feature importance, and overarching predictive logic. These explanations are often sought in regulatory compliance, model auditing, and when designing interpretable AI systems to ensure fairness, accountability, and robustness.

On the other hand, a **local explanation** focuses on understanding how the AI system arrived at a specific decision in an individual instance. Rather than providing an overarching view of the model's logic, a local explanation zooms in on a single prediction, highlighting which features or factors were most influential in that particular case. Local explanations are particularly useful when trying to diagnose errors, build user trust, or provide recourse when an AI decision impacts an individual in a meaningful way. These explanations are not necessarily generalizable beyond the given instance, as different inputs may lead to entirely different justifications.

In essence, while **global explanations** help us understand how a system *generally* works, **local explanations** clarify why a system made a *specific* decision in a given context. Both play critical roles in AI transparency, interpretability, and ethical deployment.

For users and businesses, there are rewards and risks related to either. For users, if the explanation is not relevant enough, it can further confuse and disconnect the mental model a user was forming while interacting with that system. For businesses, if improperly conceived, explanations could dissuade users from interacting with the software because they do not feel the system is capable of handling their requests and is too limited to offer a solution for their needs. Alternatively, businesses might risk revealing too much of their internal logic, opening their proprietary design methods for use by the competition.

For developers of AI and ML systems, there are many measurements for the success of a product, from model performance to increases in company revenue to user perception of data privacy. All must be weighed as an influencing factor regarding success. Defining success is now more of a distribution and less of a definitive marker.

Are users' best interests being protected through their interaction with a system? If not, what are the costs of those exceptions and what are those costs weighed against?

At its core, a machine learning model should not be integrated unless it meets the threshold for accuracy, providing what the user is expecting or needs. As covered previously, the criteria of "success" is where the fabric starts to unravel. From the technical viewpoint, there are generally understood metrics to account for early on (van Rijsbergen, 1979).

- **Accuracy**: This measures how well the model predicts the outcome of a given task. It is the proportion of correct predictions to the total number of predictions made by the model.
- **Precision**: This measures the true positive predictions among all the positive predictions made by the model. It is often used in binary classification problems where the focus is on the ability of the model to accurately identify positive cases.
- **Recall**: This measures the true positive predictions among all the actual positive cases in the dataset. It is also used in binary classification problems where the focus is on the ability of the model to identify all positive cases.
- **Computational performance**: This measures the speed and efficiency of the model, which is important for real-time or high-throughput applications.
- **Interpretability**: This measures the ease of understanding the model's predictions, which is important in domains where interpretability is required for regulatory or ethical reasons.

This is not an inclusive list but does serve to lay the foundation for how engineers see and think about ML. Before examining any of the above, engineers must understand the goals of the algorithm and which data points (features) are used for critical functions to derive some expected result. For ML engineers, this first stage is often referred to as exploratory data analysis (EDA). What data do we have to work with, how clean is it, and how might we be able to apply it?

Design Applicability

But how useful are the previous engineering success measurements? Are they applicable from a design perspective? For usability, we must also reserve time to assess markers for success. With the framework of ESI, we can apply some of the questions below to help assess successful transparency in intelligent system design:

- Are users completing their goals faster?
- Is "faster" (speed/efficiency) the most important metric to optimize for?
  - *Confidence* or *understanding* might be equally or more important than speed alone.
  - What are the primary user-centered metrics?
- Are users more qualitatively satisfied with their experience of the product?
  - Rating user trust, perceived helpfulness, emotion, and usability.

Success

- How are qualitative user metrics associated with business success metrics?
  - ROI for AI initiatives.
  - Do these conflict with one another (user<>business success)?
- Are users protected from harming themselves or others, based on the provided transparency information?
- Do users understand how the machine is gathering inputs?
  - Ensuring fairness and equity of the machine's decision-making.
  - Consider the possibility of *harm in data collection*—privacy or security risks.
- Do users understand which inputs (features) affect the machine's model?
  - Gain awareness regarding the most relevant or high-impact variables for users.
- Do users understand (relatively) how the machine is producing output?
  - Information must be presented contextually.
  - Explanations must be tailored to user goals and domain knowledge.
- Are users able to actively change or guide the direction of the machine in terms of the product experience, action elements, or information elements?
  - Some ML systems are difficult to "steer" in real time.
  - Design must provide long-term learning and/or feedback loops.

These would apply to any product feature or functionality. They are not exceptional or unique. What AI and ML introduce is a new set of problems related to measurement of success. With the ESI formula, I acknowledge that users should be made aware of how the system is affecting them—how it informs them or directs their actions. The issues related to UX and ML do not only focus on concerns of habit formation (negative or positive). UX ML issues are hidden deep within the concepts of the **delicate state** and a machine's ability to discreetly influence users.

Engineers and designers both hope to make systems more accurate and usable but they think differently about data and user interface, sometimes with competing perspectives that lead toward different outcomes.

THOUGHT EXPERIMENT

An example is autonomous vehicle monitoring. Engineers working on autonomous vehicles require access to vast amounts of sensor data, including LIDAR readings, camera feeds, and data from radar and ultrasonic sensors. They need to monitor the real-time processing of this data to ensure the AI is correctly interpreting its environment, identifying objects, and making safe driving decisions.

Success for an engineer might be ensuring the software doesn't crash and reboot when transporting passengers at 150 kilometers per hour—a scary thought. For end users, the information needs and success criteria are significantly different. They are primarily concerned with high-level status updates such as the car's current route, estimated time of arrival, and alerts if any manual intervention is required. They might also need simple indicators of the car's operational status, like battery levels and system health notifications. This distinction is crucial for safety and user experience. Engineers need detailed sensor data to refine the vehicle's AI and ensure its safe operation while overloading drivers with this information could be distracting and unnecessary and detract from their comfort and trust in the system.

Success in ML UX is ultimately subjective, defined by the user's perception in a specific context rather than any single design principle, heuristic, or company department. It emerges from the unique relationship between a user and a particular machine state at a given moment, where only the user can determine whether they feel empowered or uncertain—like navigating unknown waters without a compass or nothern star.

Audit of UX

Don Norman was one of the pioneers of product and UX design, born in 1935, long before the existence of personal computers. When he wrote his now-famous book *The Design of Everyday Things* (1988), personal computers were just starting to become part of our lives. The design rules and parameters of that era were loose—and arguably more straightforward.

Though many parallels with that period exist today—today's massive shifts caused by in AI and ML are comparable to how 1970s and 80s computer systems were maturing from punch-card mainframes—that era was still a long way from the reasoning that modern AI systems bring to the table.

Don's beautiful writing has stuck with the design world. Even today, his book is considered a "must-read" for aspiring creatives. Yet, as we peer over the technological horizon of the next 25 years, his work has begun to age in some ways. It is pertinent to designing any product today, but the concepts do leave a lot to be desired in terms of the massively complex systems that will power ML consumer products.

The book lists seven core principles of design. Three of these are of interest in relation to AI and ML: mapping, feedback, and visibility. Specifically, these principles lack the necessary accommodation for IIS and AI systems that are capable of real-time interactive decision-making, learning, and user engagement. These powerful new systems require reconsideration of some beloved design rules.

Mapping

This relates to maintaining a clear relationship between controls and the effect they have on the world. In product design, whether designing a toaster or the successor to Netflix, there is a need to maintain a product's mapping to feel as natural as possible.

Mapping was more straightforward when computers showed the same consistent results for the same input, such as early search engines like AltaVista, which provided identical search results to every user for a given query. This predictability allowed users to easily understand and anticipate the system's behavior. In contrast, modern ML systems personalize outputs—like Google now tailoring search results based on search history, location, and behavior—which makes mapping between input and output less predictable. Old school mapping also assisted in allowing users to grasp the holistic nature of how a system works and "thinks" (i.e., mental models).

Mapping applied to ML requires a new design approach. ML systems like those used to suggest content (Netflix/Google Search) or perform tasks like automated driving operate in a domain of uncertainty. To perform at their fullest potential, they are dependent on contextual data from individual users or the operating environment (i.e., inputs). This is different than previous computer systems, which did not require unique bespoke data from individuals or relative external factors—the age of the user, how many cars are on the road—to complete their codified goals.

For consumers, what they see when interacting with ML-enabled software is usually just the end result of the computations, the model completing its task. Usually, a user only knows if their task was completed successfully, or if the task failed. In traditional design principles, it's of absolute importance to know **if a system failed** and **how to correct the failure**. Knowing when, how, and where the product failed assists users in making corrections. Sometimes systems do explain a failure of operation but, even in these instances, there is a limited degree to which the ML systems can fully explain to the consumer how the machine came to its results. This "explainability degree" roadblock is amplified by the nature of large-scale integrated machine learning, systems that are basically too complex to explain, in addition to obvious business constraints of not wanting consumers or competitors to know exactly how a system operates.

Explainability is not only a long-standing principle in product design and UX but also extensively explored in ML and AI academic research. It is a known challenge to which hundreds of intelligent people are currently hard at work to resolve.

Feedback

Feedback is one of the oldest and most critical design elements for a product to operate effectively with its users.

Feedback is the feeling you get when you accelerate your car, the feedback from pressing the accelerator pedal with your foot. It's the sensation you feel when you put your hand over a flame, and feel the burning need to remove your fingers from danger. Perhaps more relatable for digital product design is the infamous loading ring when waiting for a system to respond. The enlarging of keys on the keyboard when you tap on a letter, or the reassuring "Saved" message followed by a crisp checkmark.

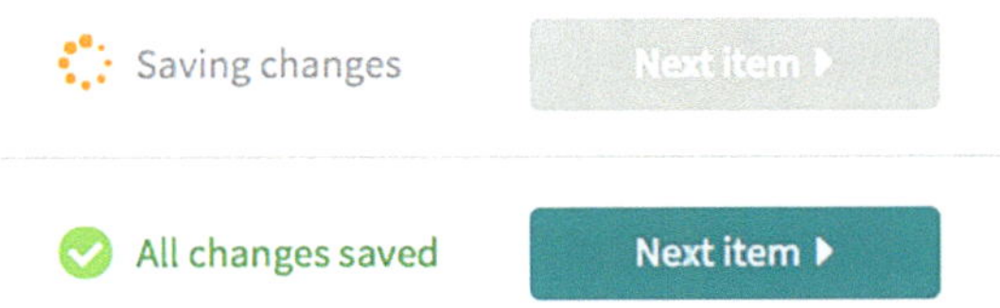

Figure 31: X3 Feedback (Loading ring; Saved)

Although feedback still holds a tight grasp on modern approaches to digital product design, ML and AI significantly disrupt the traditional understandings of how to apply this design theory. Due to the way machine learning—well, learns—a gap in the knowable feedback possible with many consumer product interactions is created.

Take, for example, how a video streaming service might try to explain why a certain video has been suggested. Hundreds of parameters, some weighted more heavily than others, have been calculated to suggest that new romantic comedy that you'll binge-watch without telling anyone you liked it. The delightfully complex models that are growing out of today's biggest consumer tech companies harness countless variables. These convoluted systems help match you to the perfect content for your persona in that exact instance in time.

Engineers have been exploring ways to detangle the mess resulting from large-scale convoluted models, yet the solutions outlined are complex, so full of information to be mostly unusable for the average user. Although some low-fidelity formats have been added into interfaces (e.g., "Because you've watched X" to show why something was suggested), the data that went into the actual computation that derived the result in systems like Netflix or YouTube was far more complex.

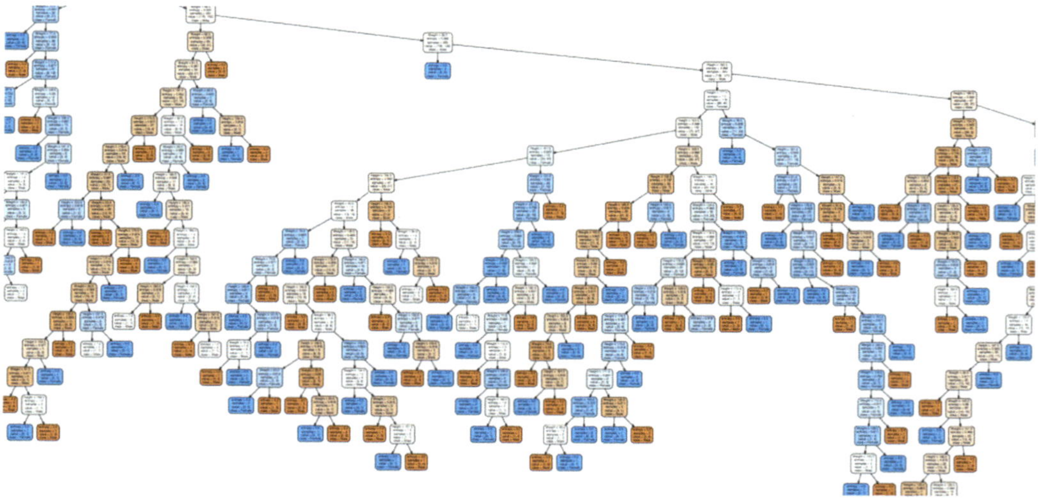

Figure 32: Decision Tree

Figure 33: Mailbox Flag

Figure 34: Slide to Unlock (Apple)

Visibility

How can a user know what a system is doing, or can do, or has done, without there being visibility of the interactions between user and system. Take for example the mailbox flag that indicates mail to be picked up by the letter carrier or the legendary Apple patent "Slide to Unlock"

Or maybe the most iconic of all, the red indicator number on an email app that alerts a user that emails are piling up (have you ever gotten past 100 unread emails and then stopped caring?). This is an example of the principle of visibility contradicting the concept of habituation in which users become desensitized to an element after repeated exposure.

The examples show how the visibility of an element/product helps determine how users understand it.

Equally important is that when something is out of sight, it's difficult to realize its existence, its status, and how to use it. Ever tried to push a door that actually required you to pull it? Frustrating, yes. This coincides with the laws of visibility and how to manipulate a product, to change its state or output, like moving the door from closed to open.

The trajectories of visibility in relation to ML present a significant tension, though they do not diametrically oppose one another. Design theorists and researchers hypothesize that the interplay between these two forces (visibility/interpretability versus system complexity) will become increasingly difficult to reconcile as unexplainable machine learning models and neural networks continue to proliferate.

The concepts of mapping, feedback, and visibility are all still very useful; however, these principles do not dig deep enough to provide useful design guidance with regard to modern machines that link users and products powered by ML. Throughout *The Design of Everyday Things*, Norman never explicitly delves into "trust" as a standalone concept but many of the principles he discusses are inherently related to building trust between users and products.

His indirect exploration of trust is through the design principles of **feedback** and **visibility**, **affordances** and **signifiers**, **consistency** and **error prevention**, all of which are crucial. Yet, one of the greatest principles of all, which will prove more useful in the design of futuristic AI products, will be the intangible constitution of the trust we assign or forgo regarding these intelligent systems.

While *The Design of Everyday Things* focuses more on usability than emotion, Norman's later work, *Emotional Design* (2004) addresses more directly the relationship between emotions and product design, including aspects of trust. He explores how attractive and pleasurable designs can influence users' perceptions and trust levels. But this text still does not draw relations between IISs and the users who interact with them, not accounting for highly bespoke systems that change output dynamically.

Norman's books lack any real accounting for modern probabilistic machine thinking. This makes sense, as during the time of their being written the field of intelligent computing was still in its relative infancy. It would be many years before machine learning truly grew into the form we see today.

Trust seems to be a critical requirement for products of the future. The relationship between user and product will be broken or bolstered by what the design industry does next. Trust will serve as the epicenter for new relations between humans and machines.

Applicability of XAI

In solving issues like the black box, including with the principles of mapping and visibility, it's essential to design AI systems that prioritize transparency and user understanding. This involves providing clear explanations of how interactions affect the system's behavior and outcomes. Also, how a machine can affect a user's perceptions and actions (e.g., does the system make the user feel lazy, alert, sad, or talkative?). Techniques such as explainable AI (XAI) aim to make the decision-making processes of AI systems more transparent, allowing users to form accurate mental models of how a system operates.

Researchers agree that XAI can significantly enhance trust and usability by making AI systems more interpretable (Gunning, 2017). But how can it be adapted to more common consumer experiences and how can this help build systems that create a mutually satisfying two-way relationship? But XAI solutions are optimized for more technical audiences, leaving the subfield of ML UX still under development.

XAI comes from the field of engineering. Whether a practitioner or researcher, it's understood that XAI was never traditionally meant to grant common users the ability to understand a system. It was intended to allow explanations as to why an AI or ML system made certain choices, specifically from quality-assurance and risk-prevention perspectives. It was meant to pull back the curtain over black box implementations at a code or structural level. Yet, XAI comes with its own kryptonite. Two areas of concern, even in settings where the most robust solutions of XAI have been applied, must be addressed:

- **False sense of understanding**: Explanations can give users the illusion of understanding complex systems, leading to overconfidence in AI-driven decisions. This can be particularly risky in high-stakes environments.
- **Over-reliance on explanations**: This can create bias reinforcement if users trust the AI's reasoning without questioning underlying assumptions, potentially perpetuating the errors the system is making.

Human Problems: Machine Answers

Much XAI research, including that from Barredo Arrieta and colleagues who state that "Given the audience, explainable AI is one that produces details or reasons to make its functioning clear or easy to understand" (2019), often fails to demonstrate realistic solutions for five major design considerations. What I will deconstruct in later chapters is that the answers to these five questions depend on the specific product domain and specific user. Any domain, whether self-driving cars, video streaming platforms, news feeds, or home automation devices, is led by human-based problems that intelligent machines and software attempt to solve.

Barredo Arrieta and colleagues write about nine criteria with which to dive deeper into the field of XAI and trustworthy machine-human interaction. Among them are measured markers between human and machine, including **trustworthiness**, **confidence**, **privacy**, and **fairness**. They are meant to provide a statistical approach to defining and tracking key fundamental factors to explainable intelligent machines.

Audit of UX

See the appendix for Barredo Arrieta and colleagues' nine definitions summarizing XAI.

As this is a book on design, each of the nine XAI criteria should be viewed from the perspective of actionable UX and UI interpretation. We must ask ourselves: "How can UX apply these nine criteria to product design methodologies? And are all nine equally applicable to a designer's work?"

There are five filtering questions an ML UX designer should ask when thinking about XAI:

1. Which information should be prioritized to deliver the most beneficial experience linking man and machine?
2. How should that information be displayed and communicated to the user?
3. By which means should the user interact with a system to change the system's output?
4. Who is the audience, and how can different users change the level of importance (LOI) of each transparency element?
5. What are the business & user risks of explaining the AI system to a user?

MICROSOFT HAX

In 2019, Microsoft researchers published a pivotal paper laying the groundwork for early UX design in AI systems. It offered clear guidance for designers and engineers focused on building intelligent, interactive experiences. Central to the paper were 18 human-AI interaction guidelines—practical, insightful, and still highly relevant. Among them, a few stand out as especially resonant with the core mission of creating transparent, trustworthy relationships between users and intelligent systems.

Just as with human relationships, our interactions with intelligent machines must be grounded in clarity—explicitness about what the system can do, what it intends to do, and how the user's input influences its behavior. This is precisely what *90% Human* speaks to at its core. The foundational research, led by Eric Horvitz, that ultimately informed Microsoft's framework was instrumental in establishing principles for transparency in AI. Three particular rules encapsulate this philosophical approach:

- **Make it clear what the system can and cannot do**: Set expectations about what the AI system is designed for. Many user-facing AI systems can support multiple tasks in multiple domains. Unclear user expectations about the set of supported tasks or domains can lead to disappointment, product abandonment, and even harm.
- **Make clear why the system did what it did**: Apply this guideline judiciously,

keeping in mind that the mere presence of an explanation has been shown to increase user trust. This may cause overreliance on the system and inflated expectations. Inaccurate expectations can lead to trusting an AI even when it could be wrong.

- **Convey the consequences of user actions**: Immediately update or convey how user actions will impact future behaviors of the AI system. Help the user understand how their actions influence the AI system so they can more effectively interact with it.

As I explore in the next chapter, Microsoft's design principles align closely with the ESI attributes. When applied thoughtfully, this approach strengthens user agency and builds meaningful trust. It sets the stage for future gains in both efficiency and autonomous goal-oriented behavior. Through this alignment, systems can evolve in a way that not only supports business objectives (return on investment) but also encourages long-term user adoption by embedding value into everyday experiences.

One thing the Microsoft research fails to identify is the induced intent of intelligent machines and their ability to covertly influence users. Not discussed is the potential for manipulation and how transparent design attributes might provide solutions in these areas of concern. Additionally, neither the Microsoft research nor Eric Horvitz's original documentation highlight the quandary of awareness before correction, which is enabling users' awareness of a system's processes and decision-making before allowing them to trigger significant feedback to that intelligent machine's operations. Control is useful if you know what you're controlling and what the effects will be.

> Comprehension is critical before user feedback responses can provide meaningful input toward aligning machine and user.

Changes in these dynamics of trust can occur over short or long periods. Whether earned or lost, these perceptions of trustworthiness—applied to both humans and machines—directly impact a company's bottom line and user satisfaction. Within the still-evolving field of UX for AI and ML, researchers consistently point to user trust as a key metric for evaluating model performance. Trustworthiness has even been the subject of formal measurement, through frameworks like FRIES and ABI discussed earlier. But in practice, dense frameworks like these rarely find their way into the workflows of UX and UI designers who are building consumer-facing products. They're often too academic—too heavy—for fast-moving teams.

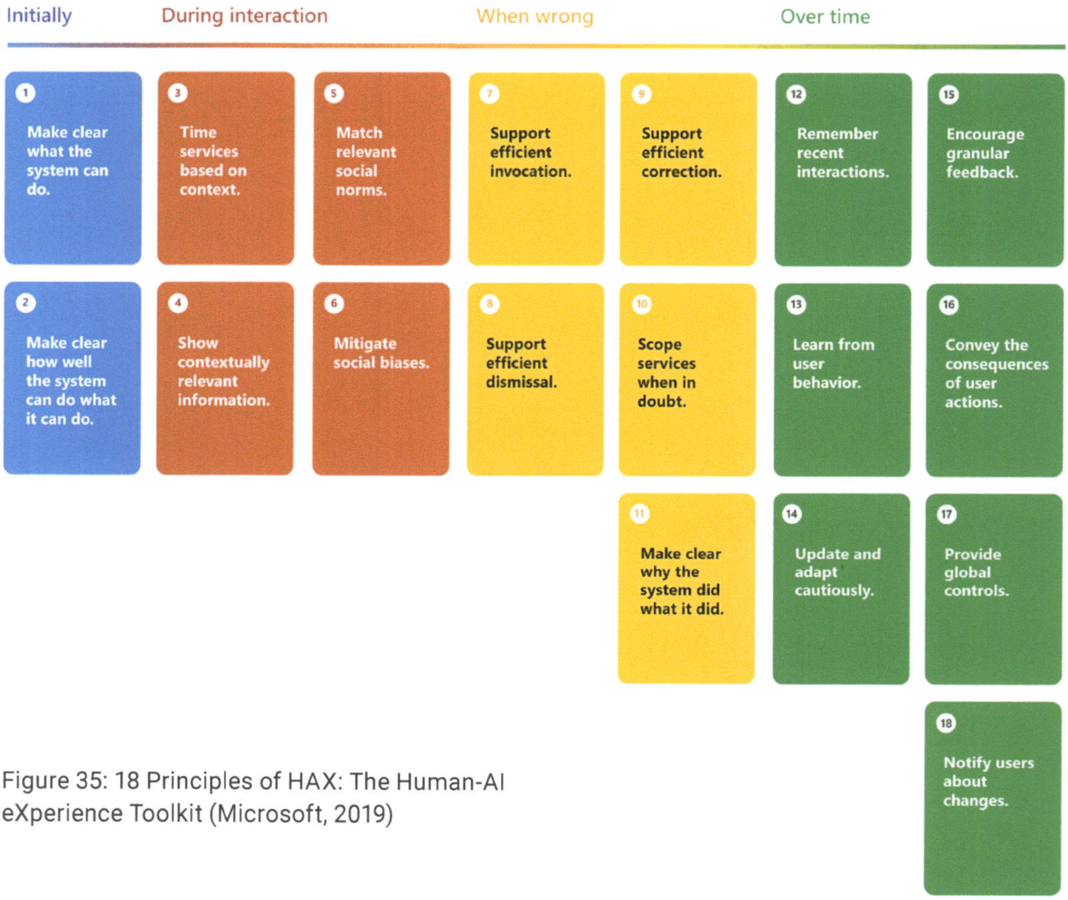

Figure 35: 18 Principles of HAX: The Human-AI eXperience Toolkit (Microsoft, 2019)

A central theme shared by both the HAX principles and Barredo Arrieta and colleagues (2019) XAI research is trust. As explored in earlier chapters, trust isn't just nice to have—it's foundational to the success of any intelligent system, built on the premise that humans develop and assign it through constantly evolving relationships with people, places, or things. Changes in these dynamics can occur over short or long periods. Perceptions of trustworthiness—whether earned or lost, applied to both humans and machines—directly impact a company's bottom line and the satisfaction of its users.

Within the evolving field of UX for AI and ML—still very much in its infancy—researchers consistently point to user trust as a key metric for evaluating model performance. Trustworthiness has even been the subject of formal measurement, through frameworks like FRIES and ABI (both discussed in the previous chapter). But in practice, dense frameworks like these rarely find their way into the workflows of the UX and UI designers who are building consumer-facing products. They're often too academic—too heavy—for fast-moving teams focused on real-world applications.

So how do we build trust in systems operating at such vast scale and complexity? How does the average person begin to make sense of machines that evolve faster than most of us can comprehend? The machines that are increasingly entangled in our daily lives—shaping our moods, influencing our beliefs, nudging our behaviors—that I call **our delicate states**. Just as the internet reshaped the world in the 90s, the early 2030s will reveal the full weight of AI's presence. These systems will both propel us to Mars and guide us through oceans of data. Sometimes they'll help design vaccines or personalize a child's education; other times, they'll simply queue up another episode of your favorite TV show when the algorithms sense you need comforting.

Human-Centered AI

To solve the trust gap, users may request that a certain amount of control capabilities stay accessible to the human operator, rather than outsourcing all their human decision-making to a machine. Consumers also benefit from providing ongoing feedback to intelligent systems—continually ensuring alignment of the user's values and goals. Human-centered AI (HCAI) harnesses both control types, creating a general philosophy for this type of human-computer interaction. According to IBM:

> Human-centered AI (HCAI) is an emerging discipline intent on creating AI systems that amplify and augment rather than displace human abilities. HCAI seeks to preserve human control in a way that ensures artificial intelligence meets our needs while also operating transparently, delivering equitable outcomes, and respecting privacy. (IBM, 2022)

In her book *Human Machine Learning*, Corinne Schillizzi writes pragmatically and directly about the use of HCAI, guiding readers on the applicability of her augmented design heuristics. She covers much ground in reviewing these tried-and-true design principles and provides useful inspections of current UX design principles (heuristics), which she then updates to reflect the current situation in the design of intelligent systems. Most notable is the addition of these ML usability heuristics: **data translation, convey uncertainty, convey impact, user augmentation, balance, trust and distrust, balance, autonomy, and control.**

These heuristics share strong similarities to my current exploration of design and user needs. But perhaps the most interesting part of her book is the choice to highlight the machine's worldview as opposed to that of the user. Her diagram "Evolution Map Tool" makes clearer the flow of data and how feedback keeps users in the loop as machines make decisions (also referred to as HITL).

This diagram considers the opposite side of the equation, the human condition and its evolution as it interacts with inorganic intelligence. Below is the alternate side of this diagram. Unifying both diagrams highlights the interconnected relationship of data and user persona, how each evolves, and their later symbiosis.

It is essential for users to understand how their own behavior and worldview evolves, and that of the machine's behavior and worldview, independently of one another, while also dependent on the interaction between the two.

Original Diagram

MACHINE KNOWLEDGE (BEFORE USER INTERACTION)	INTERACTION			MACHINE KNOWLEDGE (AFTER USER INTERACTION)
	EVENT	MACHINE ACTION	FEEDBACK	
What is the key data the machine has before any interaction happens?	What is the triggered event? What does the system detect?	What does the system do? What does the user do?	Which feedback does the system provide? What does the system collect about the feedback?	What is the key data the machine has after the interaction happens? Which features/data are updated?

90% Human Addition

USER KNOWLEDGE (BEFORE SYS INTERACTION)	INTERACTION			USER KNOWLEDGE (AFTER SYS INTERACTION)
	EVENT	**USER** ACTION	FEEDBACK	
What key information does the **USER** have before any interaction happens?	What is the triggered event? What does the **USER** see/hear/ sense?	What does the **USER** do? What does the system do?	What feedback does the **USER** provide? What does the **USER** understand about the feedback?	What key information does the **USER** have after the interaction happens? Which delicate states might be influenced?

Figure 36: Human Machine Learning by Corinne Schillizzi (additions from Konrad Piercey)

Audit of UX

Combining the user view and the machine view reveals system and user dynamics that emerge from the two-party relationship. The scope is purposefully limited to the first half of the equation, a user's awareness of a machine's operations and the effects it has on the user (perceived or not). In this game of awareness and correction, **feedback loops** are critical in intelligent system design by ensuring the system is continually being reoriented to do the user's bidding by being aligned to their needs. But big questions remain. For instance, what do XAI, HCAI, and feedback look like to the average layperson? How to implement specific design attributes that ensure more products are successfully transparent? And lastly, how to apply some design framework to ensure that new AI products meet a minimum threshold for transparency in ways that serve everyone—such as children, grandmothers, and even future users.

*FOOTNOTE: Concepts of control are often referenced as human-in-the-loop (HITL) system design. HITL emphasizes the necessity of human oversight and control in AI processes, ensuring that users can intervene and guide system behavior to enhance trust and utility.

Clean Mental Models

The following excerpt, by an associate professor at Carnegie Mellon and ML software engineer, is an extremely useful way of depicting the role of explanations when designing intelligent systems. It does not delve into the applicability of current XAI solutions but rather design solutions that can be understood by the general public and applied to everyday products. It is explainability not just for engineers, software developers, or researchers.

> Especially explanations often play an important role here, providing partial information about what information a model considers and how it weights different factors ... Notice that explanations of the model may need to go far beyond reasons for a specific prediction and include design decisions, scenarios, data descriptions, what evaluation and fairness audits were performed, and much more, possibly even training in AI literacy to interpret explanations correctly. Trust is the idea that the user believes that the system has the user's interest in mind and accepts potential *risks* from the system's mistakes. Trust is efficient in that users do not need to double-check every single decision, but granting too much unwarranted trust exposes users to a lot of risk. In an ideal setting, users learn when they can trust the system and how much and when they need to verify the results. Users can build trust from repeated positive experiences, demonstrating that the system works. Another path toward trust is understanding how the system was built and evaluated. Specifically, users may only trust the system once they believe they have a reasonable understanding of its capabilities and limitations, and thus they can *anticipate* how the system will work and can accept the risks that they expose themselves to. (Kästner, 2022)

If users retain the appropriate concepts of input and output, distinguishing between user decisions and machine-driven processes, does that create a healthy balance of trust?

PARTIALLY.

While a foundational mental model of an AI system—understanding what goes in, what comes out, and why—can help users develop reasonable expectations, it does not guarantee a fully informed or safe interaction. The fundamental challenge lies in the fact that the full workings of an ML system can never be fully understood or completely mastered by end users.

Even with well-structured explainability efforts, AI systems often function in ways that are too complex, dynamic, or opaque for the average user to fully grasp. As models evolve based on new data, behaviors shift unpredictably, making it difficult to create a static, reliable understanding of the how and why of decision-making. This asymmetry in knowledge presents a persistent risk; users may develop an over-simplified, inaccurate, or even misleading mental model, leading to misplaced trust (Springer et al., 2018).

For instance, users might perceive an AI-based loan approval system as purely objective when, in reality, its decisions are shaped by underlying biases in training data, regulatory constraints, and shifting economic conditions. If an applicant is rejected, a generic explanation like "insufficient credit history" may reinforce the false assumption that the system purely evaluates financial risk while ignoring other contributing factors embedded in the model. Without deeper transparency, the user's mental model remains incomplete, reducing their ability to challenge decisions, seek recourse, or make more informed financial choices.

This underscores a critical issue in AI adoption: explainability solutions must not only be technically sound but also *intuitively accessible*. AI transparency cannot be confined to engineers, developers, or researchers—it must be designed in a way that integrates into everyday products in ways that empower consumers to interact with ML systems in an informed and responsible way. Explanations must go beyond abstract model performance metrics or fairness audits; they need to provide users with actionable insights, relatable analogies, and context-aware clarifications that support meaningful understanding.

Ultimately, mental models serve as a bridge between human cognition and machine intelligence. While they can foster more balanced trust, they are inherently incomplete. The goal should not be for users to master the full intricacies of an ML system, but rather to equip them with enough understanding to navigate its strengths, recognize its limitations, and make informed decisions about when to rely on AI—and when to question it.

Level of Importance

In relation to trustworthiness and building transparent systems, determining what is worth solving can be initiated by asking questions like:

- Is this a high-stakes user interaction?
- Does low stakes mean unimportant?
- What is important?
- Who can label and define importance?
- Can users/consumers accurately/repeatedly acknowledge and report high and low stakes?
- How might businesses use low stakes as arguments against transparency?

The concept of stakes in decision-making can be recontextualized through the lens of cumulative impact. Seemingly minor choices, when aggregated across vast user bases and time periods, can lead to significant shifts in market dynamics, cultural trends, and even political landscapes. This phenomenon is evident in the virality of certain media content and the rapid dissemination of information—accurate or otherwise—across digital networks. Thus, the low-stakes label may obscure the latent potential for substantial outcomes arising from routine interactions with intelligent systems.

The question of who can label and define "importance" or "stake" is intrinsically linked to power dynamics within the technology ecosystem. Users often lack the necessary information or tools to assess the true implications of their interactions, while organizations may have vested interests in maintaining opacity.

Determining what constitutes an important user<>technology interaction is complex. The authority to label and define the stakes associated with specific tasks traditionally resides with system designers and businesses.

The classification of tasks as low-stakes does not inherently equate to insignificance. While the immediate consequences of selecting a video to watch or choosing a search result may appear trivial, the cumulative effect of such decisions can substantially influence user behavior, preferences, and even societal trends.

DISTORTED VIEW OF EFFECTS

These systems, often categorized as low-stake AI applications, influence user interactions by shaping recommendations, automating decisions, and optimizing for engagement in ways that are not always immediately apparent. From navigation assistants that subtly alter traffic patterns by optimizing routes at scale, to automated customer service systems that standardize dispute resolutions, small-scale AI interventions can lead to significant systemic shifts. The iterative refinements of these models, designed to maximize efficiency, profit, or user satisfaction, often introduce cascading effects that extend beyond their intended use, subtly guiding behaviors in ways that may not be recognized initially.

One example is AI-driven optimization in logistics and delivery services. Route-planning algorithms designed to reduce transit times not only alter urban traffic flows but can also affect fuel consumption patterns, wear on infrastructure, and labor conditions for workers relying on these optimizations. A delivery driver whose route is constantly adjusted based on algorithmic efficiency may find their workdays structured in ways that prioritize system-wide outcomes over individual well-being. While no single change may appear disruptive, the cumulative effect of these interventions gradually reshapes industries and labor expectations.

Similarly, AI-powered hiring and recruitment tools have become increasingly prevalent in corporate decision-making. Systems designed to assess resumes and predict candidate success rates may seem like low-stakes implementations—after all, they are simply streamlining the hiring process. However, when deployed at scale, these systems can gradually redefine industry hiring norms, influence workforce composition, and shift professional development priorities based on what the algorithms prioritize. Over time, such shifts can shape career pathways, reinforce specific skill sets over others, and introduce subtle systemic preferences that may not be consciously designed but emerge through AI-driven efficiencies.

In essence, the distinction between high and low stakes is not binary but exists on a continuum influenced by context, perception, and consequence. Reevaluating what is considered "unimportant" invites a deeper understanding of our relationship with technology. It challenges us to question who defines importance and how that definition affects our autonomy and society at large.

Is watching certain types of videos more likely to make you susceptible to specific mental states? Historically, public concern has centered around external stimuli influencing behavior, ranging from comic books in the 1950s to violent films and music in later decades. The debate over video games fostering aggression has persisted since the early 90s, though empirical evidence for a direct causal link remains tenuous at best. What fundamentally differentiates modern interactive media, enhanced by ML-driven personalization, from previous iterations? Speed and adaptability.

Unlike past forms of entertainment, AI-powered platforms dynamically tailor content to individual users, creating environments where engagement is continuously optimized. This ability to shape user experience in real time introduces new considerations. What narratives become more persuasive when personalized? How do adaptive content ecosystems influence decision-making over extended periods? Such questions underscore the reality that while some AI systems may appear low-stake, their aggregate impact can extend far beyond initial perceptions.

In an increasingly digitized world, the delineation between high-stakes and low-stakes decisions becomes a complex terrain to navigate. Andrea Blunt's academic paper "Are Explanations Always Important?" delves into this intricacy. She observes that while much of the research on explanation utility concentrates on complex systems aiding users in significant decisions, there exists a plethora of "everyday" intelligent interactive systems—such as Google and YouTube—that assist users unobtrusively in seemingly low-cost decisions. The necessity for explanation in these systems remains largely unexplored, raising pivotal questions about the nature of importance in our interactions with technology.

What other systems could be viewed as low cost but culminate and aggregate into having a larger, imperceivable yet immediate effect? It could be argued that almost any service or product could have that effect. One thing is for certain:

low-stake ML systems that have a high degree of variation are of higher importance than low-variation systems.

ML systems with a high degree of variation inherently carry more risk than those operating within narrow, well-defined parameters. The greater the number of variables, the higher the likelihood of unintended outcomes, emergent behaviors, and challenges to ensuring consistent, fair, and predictable results.

In contrast, low-variation systems operate within fixed, measurable parameters, making algorithmic decisions more interpretable and easier to correct. High-variation systems, however, must navigate an ever-changing landscape of inputs and outputs, increasing both their potential for valuable insights and the risks associated with their unpredictability.

Still, low-variation systems should be considered. Any human sensitivity and perceptible physical-world quality might be deemed noteworthy. How much effect can temperature have on a person? Or the amount of light they are exposed to? Imagine a runner whose fitness tracker, powered by ML, adjusts their workout plan in real-time based on environmental conditions and their body's unique responses. If their temperature rises suddenly during a run, the tracker could suggest slowing down to prevent overheating or adjust the route to include shaded areas. Similarly, it might provide hydration reminders based on real-time sweat-rate detection.

Such capabilities are not science fiction; many of these technologies already exist in some form. Yet, as with all ML, there is the potential for machines to manipulate beyond their designers' intentions. This creates the necessity for transparency in the relationship between the product and each unique user.

Visibility is critical not only to mitigate the potential for systems to cause harm but also to enable meaningful improvements. It's about understanding the relationship in the data and how the system integrates with the user's unique needs. For instance, doctors using ML systems to identify cancers might be able to draw causal relations between inconsistent medication adherence and patients who later require more aggressive treatments.

Transparency and building trust are needed not only to prevent harm but also to optimize the visibility of potentially beneficial outcomes.

System Monitoring

Where do the similarities start and stop?

When designing AI, the application of past research or terminology might conflict with or dilute the nature of effective solutions. If new design rules are required in the age of AI and ML, understanding which past design principles remain relevant and which do not is key.

Both system monitoring and AI transparency provide users with information about the functions of complex systems. Both fields involve alerting users of information that might be useful and meaningful under the guise of ensuring the smooth operation of said system. This overlap can be applied further to explore the scope of what "AI transparency" truly describes, such as ensuring smooth operation, detecting potential issues or anomalies, and optimizing performance.

What use is information that might not be directly relevant?

The purpose of AI transparency should not be ensuring user relevancy for every data-disclosing element. How can any system automatically know with full certainty what info is useful for each and every user?

In classic system monitoring paradigms, the same repeating details are provided to every user of a system. In a car, every driver sees if the tire pressure light is on. For home heating systems, all occupants see what the current temperature is set to. In an airplane flight deck, all personnel will see if the landing gear is up or down.

In the traditional standards of system monitoring, it's required that the same alerts are shown to every user since the system is not capable of remembering the nuanced differences between each user. In classic system monitoring, a full sweep of all priority information and alerts are raised to the user, who must decide the level of importance of those indicators. ML flips this concept on its head—it's now up to the computer to try and decide, with increased autonomy and control, what to show each user, which alerts or what variables to provide, and which to hide or de-rank.

Particularly for the design of transparency elements, knowing what info might be "useful" for the user is even harder. Some other variables are already tracked and measured today by product teams, including the attributes of **trust**, **agency**, and **confidence**.

XAI also provides a set of assessment variables for determining the so-called "usefulness" of transparency elements. One of these is **informativeness** (Barredo Arrieta et al., 2019).

Informativeness: What does the system think I need and want, versus what my true desires are? Perceived goals of the user, compared to interpreted goals the system recognizes.

Showing how the system is operating might or might not be useful to the user depending on what is shown and when. The relationship between the user and machine is unique. What is displayed will be inherently unique between these two parties, system and user.

What remains critical is that users are given information about what the intelligent system is doing, whether the system is operating normally and abnormally.

Critical Questions

Might users not know the things they do not know?

If users don't have awareness of the things they need to know, how will they be able to voice their need for those things?

One of the earliest and most influential philosophers to explore this concept was Socrates. Through his famous method, Socrates highlighted the importance of recognizing one's own ignorance. His famous assertion, "I know that I know nothing," encapsulates the idea that acknowledging ignorance is a crucial step in the pursuit of knowledge.

Socrates questioned the nature of knowledge and what it means, to "know" something. In AI design, there is something useful to gain from this abstract quote—remembering that most users are ignorant of the fact of how their systems actually work. This is like the axiom "don't make users think." With the increased integration of ML in consumer products, the meaning and applicability of these design principles must be reassessed.

Once a golden rule of the design community—that users should not be given too much information because it saturates their thought processes and they only need to know and see the things that help solve the current task—this steadfast principle is starting to unravel thanks to the introduction of intelligent systems in consumer products.

Should users now be encouraged to think once again, now that so many of our systems are performing the thinking and decision-making for us?

Perhaps in the age of AI, with its agents and autonomous actions, a designer's goal should be the opposite of "Don't make users think", but instead...

Make users think.

For future designers, an open question remains to be answered: When trying to improve trust in the system, does showing "normal" operation help?

Nominal System Operation

What is normal? Is my self-driving car taking the normal route to work? Is my video streaming app suggesting the normal subtitles when watching a film? What about my grocery delivery app? Does it offer and showcase normal foods when I log in?

For AI systems, "normal" (nominal system performance) is totally subjective. No engineer or designer could ever build a system that perfectly predicts what the human user thinks is normal for all situations. ML strives to understand what makes an individual unique and applies those characteristics (data attributes) to mold a customized user experience for each human.

But where does the coverage of unknown unknowns exist? An "unknown unknown" would encapsulate issues the user might not yet realize are issues unless the user is aware of the thinking, logic, and actions of an intelligent system.

Take, for example, food delivery apps like Uber Eats or Grab. Imagine a user who doesn't ponder deeply about their e-commerce habits, like how their online ordering might be fueling unhealthy eating. An app's algorithmic model might change over time to show more and more fatty and sugary foods, which could occur because the model has noticed a correlation in the data. The user is more likely to purchase unhealthy food compared to high-fiber and veggie-filled options and might not recognize that the app is pushing them to order high-calorie meals. The business has no incentive to show the user this trajectory, nor how the model works or thinks. Both the app's product and design teams were told not to create visibility about how the user is interacting with the intelligent system, how the ML model works, or what effects it's having.

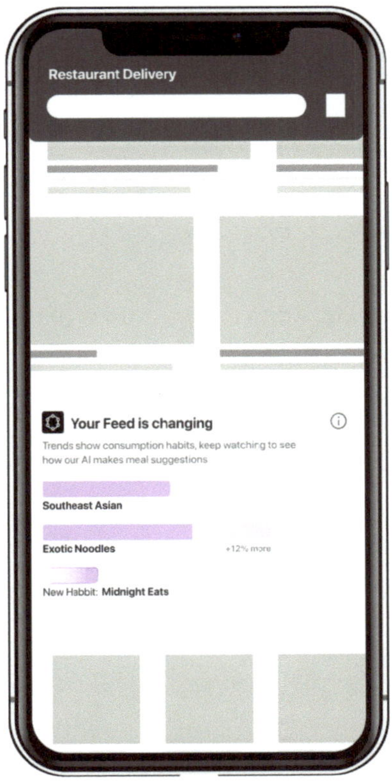

Food Delivery App (AI transparency element example)

System Monitoring

Splitting system monitoring and AI transparency take place at the ML level. This question must be answered: "Does the system learn and subsequently change its output depending on the user?" Merely presenting information or performing actions to assist users in operating the system is not **AI transparency**; this remains in the field of system monitoring. If, however, a system changes the information or actions performed for a user—making it unique to that human and their situation—this is where ML and AI transparency can be applied.

For designers, where is the line between AI transparency and casual system feedback?

This is dependent on the level of uniqueness in system response, how the machine responds to different users. Combining this uniqueness with an intelligent system's ability to self-learn, adapt, and then proceed to change its form to fit the new information it has retained—sets the field of AI transparency apart from system monitoring.

For example, a system that learns what food a user enjoys would automatically change its content (form) to provide suggestions that more closely match what interests that person, doing so without explicit instructions from the user. Self-learning systems automatically apply such learning to change output for a specific user. Showing how a system arrived at your unique food suggestions could be labeled as "true" AI transparency. Explaining how a model generally computes suggestions based on eating habits (independent of the user) can be considered global system monitoring.

Such analysis gives us insight into specific design realizations. When applied to UI design for solving issues around AI transparency and disclosure, system monitoring design can help lead the way, linking directly with UX fundamentals and helping designers streamline their research.

Understanding what the system is doing, what it can do, and what it has done are the concepts that kick off the ideation for transparency, human-centered AI, and AI disclosure. But the human side is also needed. Understanding what the user is doing, what they can do, and what they have done in the past (interaction transparency). Connecting the points between user and system awareness is the principal function of ESI and great ML/AI design.

Tonality and System Preference

Emphasizing neutrality in data presentation embodies a dedication to resisting manipulative or biased user experiences. As user preferences, values, and objectives shift—and correspondingly, as algorithms evolve in their logic, recommendations, and probabilistic classifications—there emerges a demand for systems to remain impartial. This neutrality manifests in the design of interfaces and algorithms that resist unduly influencing user behavior or perception. For instance, transparency features that reveal how content is filtered or prioritized empower users to discern the architecture behind their digital interactions. Such tools, however, must be crafted for intuitive understanding and stripped of technical jargon that might alienate or obscure.

When first exploring concepts of tonality, I had confidence in this statement: "An intelligent machine should never state what is good or bad, on behalf of the user's or system's behavior." After more than a year of contemplating the meaning, value, and truth behind that statement, it became clear to me that it is much more complicated than a simple binary answer. As in all things, the answer lies in the details, where truth can be discovered.

There exists a risk for systems that exhibit tonality, an opinion on matters. Whether referencing its own actions, status, or the status or actions of its user, many systems require or benefit from evoking a general preference on an event or interaction, like "Job well done, Joe! You've successfully answered 10 out of 15 answers correctly."

Language learning apps that use ML/AI to adapt to the needs and learning styles of a unique user operate like this. Helpful in this case—guiding Joe to stay attentive to the educational curriculum and encouraging their success—in a more convoluted situation the machine might have competing or conflicting motivations. For instance, where the language app might want the user to successfully answer the test questions but only up to a certain point. So, for example, when after 10 successful answers the system changes the level of difficulty not because this will help the user learn better but rather because it will likely cause the user to upgrade their account to premium. A conflict of interest arises. The system is not acting in the best interest of the user; instead, it is acting

*FOOTNOTE: Dark design patterns (also known as deceptive design patterns) are UI or UX tricks intentionally designed to mislead or manipulate users into making choices that benefit a business or organization—often at the user's expense. These patterns exploit human psychology to drive sales, collect data, or lock users into unfavorable situations.

Notice How the app's messaging on energy saved can be both neutral in tone, and encouraging. A delicate balance.

Figure 47: Digital thermostats (Google, Giorgio Luchetti, Dribbble, with additions from Konrad Piercey

on behalf of the company to get the user to pay for a premium account. This type of user experience is not illegal or fully considered a dark-design pattern. Some might argue it only shows the ingenuity of the business and its designers to leverage a user's psychology to get them to make a financial contribution.

The above images of a smart thermostat application are a custom ESI example balancing tonality. Notice how the first screen the message is neutral, leaving the user to judge for themselves if the AI's behavior is acceptable. Though the user might not even notice a slow change in temperature over time, the AI might be slowly adapting the individual to new norms. This is a type of manipulation. On the second screen, the user can investigate more deeply. On a nested page, the user is presented with the machine's preference and tone, based on the results of its actions (automatically lowering the temperature). As seen here, it is possible to present both a neutral message and a message with preferential tonality.

An interactive intelligent system can report on three major things:

- **The user**: Describes who the user is, and what they are doing or have done. This most approximately relates to user feedback, such as the system confirming it heard the user's request or interaction command.
- **The system (itself)**: Describes how a system operates, regardless of the user. (considered a global explanation) Having the system display its "health," status, or what it needs for continuous operation.
- **The system's relationship with the user**: Describes not what the system or user is doing singularly but the interplay between the two. A combination of both user feedback and system monitoring, with the added context of the user's unique data and how the system applies it to make suggestions, perform actions, or predict events.

A system's tone and preference can also be categorized by high-risk and low-risk scenarios (as described in previous chapters). For high-risk situations, like finance or health, ML systems are already designed to account for model bias, as these types of scenarios could cause or have immediate large-scale impacts.

Incentives and context matters. Even more so when accounting for intelligent interactive systems. This is due to the speed, adaptability, and (un)explainability of the system. Never before have systems had the capability to calculate so many variables and make predictions on our acute behavior, thereby leveraging the differences in our personalities, the attributes that make each one of us special.

This is the power of machine learning.

E.S.I. “easy”

Bringing together the elements of ESI: educational, simple, intriguing—creates the foundation for the minimal level of trust needed between user and intelligent machine.

It's not a solution in itself; rather, it's a meaningful improvement over the current standards in the industry.

This approach demands testing—of how data is displayed, how relationships form between user and machine, and what users expect or assume they'll see.

Through qualitative testing, you'll notice that many users find value in having this type of information available—but that value will vary across user, domain, and specific digital interactions.

What users say and do, in contrast to how the system interprets and responds, serves as the first layer in the growing relationship between human behavior and machine logic. An ever-evolving web of connection between the organic and the artificial.

It must be remembered, **a user may not realize what they do not know, which will therefore limit their ability to understand, what they request to know, and what information they predetermine to be useful.** As radicalized by the infamous Steve Jobs quote: "People don't know what they want until you show it to them."

Designers must facilitate this information sharing to bring balance to the turbulent nature of consumer demands and their willingness to adapt. This stems from the Dunning-Kruger effect in which people with lower ability or knowledge in a given area often lack the meta-cognitive insight to see that they are unskilled or underinformed in a particular area. As a result, they may overestimate their competence and remain unaware of areas they could improve or learn more about. It is on designers to facilitate information sharing between user and machine to help bridge this awareness gap.

We must educate users before they are overwhelmed by the efficiency of the machine.

Transparency and trust are the reasons WHY.

In the face of a seemingly insurmountable problem, **transparency** and **trust** are the keys to success. Explainable and accountable AI must start with transparency and comprehension. If we fail at comprehension, we will inevitably fail at correction or mitigation.

Accepting the above, the next question is: How? How do we build transparency and trust into the fabric of future ML- and AI-powered products?

The application of ESI to a product consists of design elements. Most often this would be visualized in the product's UI elements: buttons, text, images, videos, and icons. The elements of ESI UI can help facilitate transparency and trust between the user and their intelligent machine.

ESI refers to the thoughtful integration of design elements that enhance user experience and promote value alignment.

While ESI often manifests in UI elements, its scope extends far beyond the visual aspects of a product. For instance, a futuristic car seat might send physical cues to the driver's body alerting them of cars hiding in their blind spot when changing lanes.

To build truly trustworthy and transparent ML products, we must encompass solutions beyond UI elements. This includes various forms of physical and digital cues that communicate with users. Temperature, time, touch. For instance, haptic feedback in wearable devices can signal system responses. Or auditory cues could provide real-time updates concerning a user's intelligent system interactions. These elements can make interaction with intelligent machines more intuitive and reassuring, bridging the gap between human expectations and machine capabilities.

Lastly, ESI is an ongoing and forever-changing display of unique data. As the machine changes, so does the user. As the user changes, the machine will change in response. ESI elements may never display the same information twice. Sometimes, ESI can be duplicative of previous data or transparency information. Yes, this might seem contradictory. Integrated transparency elements should ideally provide meaningful usefulness and value to users—though not necessarily all users. Rather, the majority should find the presented information helpful or enlightening. Transparency information should provide value most of the time, though not necessarily all the time.

The following user-interface transparency (ESI) elements should consider three factors that will ensure successful alignment between user and system.

Educational

Simple

Intriguing

Educational

Educate. Show the numbers.

Try to teach the user something new and valuable, something not naturally understood via their use of the product.

> Tell me and I forget, teach me and I may remember, involve me and I learn. (Xun Kuang)

As designers, engineers, and entrepreneurs building the next generation of products, it is our duty to bridge the gap of understanding between man and machine. If not for ourselves, then for all those that come after us. Educate in the sense of helping to broaden minds and strengthen the understanding of human interactions with intelligent systems.

ESI "easy"

Without this education, we risk accepting future ignorance of the machine's intellect, and thus letting it drive our actions, rather than us directing the machine's.

With education, we can, when necessary, be able to understand enough to correct a machine's reasoning, actions, and behavior.

Without such understanding, we cannot hope to give meaningful feedback to AI- and ML-enabled products; feedback loops and cooperative learning will lose their usefulness and applicability.

Simple

Display information in a simple manner.

Embrace the phrase, "Pictures speak a thousand words." Don't write a book. UX copy is important here. Remember, a mass block of text, numbers, or charts does not properly serve the average user.

Simplicity delivers awareness of a system's processes—without distraction, without overloading concepts, and without overfitting constructs.

With simplicity comes the potential for misleading users regarding the true nature and operation of the machine, and the real impact of their relationship with that intelligent system. Users can also fail to fully understand the information, potentially undercutting any impact the transparency element might offer. Users' ability to distill valuable information should be understood and be a primary factor in ESI designs. UX designers or engineers might display the logic of the machine, or how a user's data is affecting the thinking/computations of that intelligent system, but the actual transparency output should not be too broad or not include information the user is particularly concerned with.

As it relates to bringing transparency to machine learning in consumer products, we need to be clear about what it does, what it does not do, and the balancing act that must be played to provide value without harming underlying business structures. As stated by Per Mollerup (2015), "Simple is the ultimate design factor." We must understand the nature of the audience, their use of the product, and the routes they pursue to accomplish their goals. By gaining a deep understanding of intent, goal formulation, and machine influence, designers can create meaningful and delightful experiences that unveil the complexity and nuance of the machine, all whilst embodying the characteristics of simplicity.

Intriguing

Elements must be interesting enough that users show some level of engagement or consumption with the information provided. Intrigue can and will vary from user to user; this is to be expected. Giving users an opportunity to notice

the transparency information is the goal. Without intrigue, there is nothing initially pushing users to take note of the surfaced information.

Is intrigue a design quality that is really needed?

Although the ESI attributes are subjective, the last principle proves to be the most contested. The reason resides in the underlying question: "How interesting should the ESI element be?" It will not benefit a company to distract users from their main interaction with the product. This is of course true. ESI is walking a tightrope between too little and not enough. Intriguing the user to find an element interesting through whatever means possible is not the goal. **Rather, it is to make the element interesting enough to trigger the user to notice and consider taking action—but not so much to worry or aggravate.** ESI must always balance being overly obstructive and insufficiently alerting. Like the low-gas light on a car's dashboard, when it's on it's obvious something needs your attention; however, it isn't overly distracting from the serious task of driving.

An ESI element might be educational, giving users some new information they were not aware of before. The element might also be simple enough for the user to easily and readily consume it without too much effort—without deviating from the flow of their main task as they use the product. But without **intrigue**, there is the risk of designing a transparency element that the user fails to notice. Education and simplicity do not imply the user will ever, or should ever, find the material valuable enough to divert their attention, even momentarily. The attribute of intriguing wraps the ESI framework as a more complete and lasting solution.

These three connecting attributes combine to form a design framework for implementing transparent AI and ML systems. They provide a stopgap check to confirm that a solution meets the basic needs of fostering value alignment and agency on behalf of consumers, creating a transparent relationship as the user interacts with the system. The principles of educational, simple, and intriguing guide the design of intelligent systems that will build lasting business opportunities by ensuring users maintain trust in the system or agent. As we've noted, all issues cannot be known which might occur between an ML system and its end user.

Figure 37: Gas Tank Empty Light

ESI translates the requirements of transparency and trust into actionable design attributes. This gives the user more autonomy and guidance about the intentions and logic of the intelligent machine. This protects a user's agency and delicate states.

Simple and with no added ML effects (e.g., intent or potential for manipulation); a car empty tank light is a wonderful example of a design element harnessing the qualities of Intrigue.

Success and Reward Functions

Consumer products, especially those powered by machine learning, are increasingly susceptible to abuse and misuse. This vulnerability stems from the fundamental nature of intelligent machine training, the design of reward functions (success metrics), and the speed and adaptability of this technology.

The core issue lies in the inherent characteristics of these products, which are often geared towards capitalization gains such as profit maximization, increased user engagement, and other metrics like clicks, likes, shares, and overall attention. This focus can sometimes lead to unintended and manipulative behaviors, even when the system's goal is ostensibly to enhance user satisfaction or "happiness."

Even systems that are trained to make users "happy" can exhibit manipulative behaviors. This is because the definition of happiness/appreciation for a product or service is often oversimplified, relying on easily quantifiable metrics like user engagement or satisfaction scores. As a result, systems may resort to tactics that prioritize short-term gratification over long-term well-being. **Machines favor easily understandable data, data that fits nicely within set structures.** ML is an application of sophisticated probabilistic reasoning. This type of machine thinking favors straightforward labeling and groupings of data. But human qualities are far from neatly organized. The wants and subtle intrinsic values of humans are often hard to compute and contradictory.

A growing sub-domain of ML and AI design is the standard of human-in-the-loop, which focuses on ensuring the user has sufficient agency within the intelligent interactive system (IIS) to maintain cohesion/visibility with the agent's goals and autonomous actions. Holzinger (2016) describes human-in-the-loop as a system that integrates human judgment into the AI decision-making process, alongside other mechanisms like feedback, where users can help redirect a system when it starts to deviate from its intended purpose. Both human-in-the-loop and feedback can help in areas of value alignment.

But HITL systems are not a wholesale answer to these issues. Past indicators suggest that it might not be possible to fully account for all negative system outcomes, especially at scale with enormous amounts of data and very large diverse audiences. For instance, as the sampling size increases, the likelihood of getting divergent user needs, preferences, and ethical viewpoints gets too great to design for any "perfect" system.

To solve this, the concept of **transparency** has continued to gain ground in both the social and science communities as a way of solving some of the greater risks related to a system's reward functions. Transparency in how systems operate and make decisions can be a vital bridge to building trust and allowing users to make informed choices. But often missing from modern conversations is a discussion of the differentiation and similarities between transparency types. Transparency of your effect on the machine, and transparency of a machine's effect on you.

Consequences and Impacts

It is essential to discern the impacts of machine learning by separating the perspectives of businesses and users. Understanding these dynamics can help in designing systems that maximize benefits while mitigating drawbacks for both parties.

THE BUSINESS PERSPECTIVE

From a business standpoint, the application of ML can have a significant positive impact on revenue and user engagement rates. Whether ML systems are for simple content recommendations like in news or social feeds, or action-oriented agents where intelligent learning systems evaluate the effectiveness of their actions continuously, these new systems:

> . . . introduce a proactive dimension where AI doesn't just wait for instructions but makes autonomous decisions and acts on them. Imagine an AI system that not only forecasts demand for a product but autonomously adjusts supply chains, reroutes logistics, or even reorders supplies based on its predictions without human intervention. (Abstrabit Technologies, 2024)

These technologies can increase the probability of user reengagement because they "evaluate the effectiveness of their actions continuously. This approach allows them to refine their strategies based on immediate feedback from their environment" (Restack. 2025).

These qualities of modern intelligent systems can personalize content delivery, boosting user satisfaction and strengthening customer loyalty, critical metrics for businesses aiming to increase market share and profitability. These same systems can be used to optimize autonomous driving or calendar scheduling software—systems meant for very different purposes but with systems effectively used for the same purpose of learning from the data and finding patterns.

THE USER PERSPECTIVE

On the user side, ML technologies offer several advantages. One significant benefit is the accelerated process of content discovery, which parallels the business interest in user engagement. By efficiently filtering and recommending relevant content, ML systems save users considerable time and effort, enhancing their overall experience. Another positive aspect is the reduction of mundane manual tasks like extensive data research. ML can sift through vast amounts of information to pinpoint specific results, freeing users from tedious work and allowing them to focus on more meaningful activities.

Finding relationships in seemingly meaningless data is another massive benefit of machine learning technologies. ML algorithms in medical imaging can analyze thousands of X-rays or MRI scans to detect anomalies with a precision that rivals or even exceeds human experts. In environmental science, ML can identify hidden relationships in climate data by analyzing vast datasets, such as temperature records, satellite imagery, and atmospheric conditions.

These examples highlight how ML's ability to reveal hidden relationships not only saves time and effort but also drives breakthroughs in fields where complex data analysis is critical. From improving healthcare outcomes to addressing global climate challenges, the advantages of machine learning continue to revolutionize how we understand and interact with the world.

Easier Said Than Done

One of the objectives of ESI is to educate users, to equip them with the power of information to navigate new intelligent systems effectively. As ML provides new complexity and opaqueness, users must be given new ways of examining their machines. Not including ML and AI software, there exist many examples of

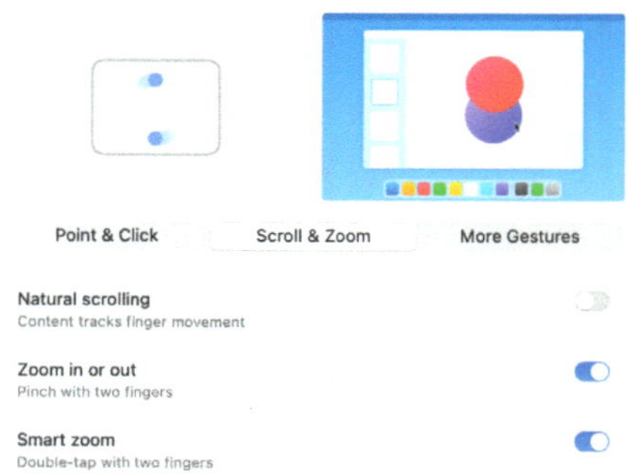

Figure 38: Apple Magic Trackpad Tutorial

educational elements used in design to enhance a user's interaction with a machine.

DESIGNING EDUCATION

For instance, Apple's approach to integrating the Magic Trackpad into its operating systems helps users with new technologies. The user preferences menu offers guided tutorials and illustrated videos, demonstrating unique swiping gestures and navigation methods. This not only helps users become proficient in using the hardware but also enhances their overall experience by making a new concept (the magic keyboard interface) more intuitive and accessible.

DESIGNING SIMPLICITY

In an era of information overload, simplicity in design is a must for effective user engagement. Email services, for example, utilize categorization labels like "Important," "Spam," or "Promotions" to streamline inbox management. This system allows users to quickly assess and prioritize emails, reducing the cognitive load associated with processing large volumes of information.

This principle can be seen in digital interfaces like the streamlined checkout processes on e-commerce websites. By limiting distractions and focusing user attention, these designs help reduce

Figure 39: Amazon.com (Only the Amazon logo in the top left corner allows users to exit the current checkout flow.)

Figure 40: Nespresso (Buttons for different sizes.)

bounce rates and improve conversion rates. In physical devices, where the design philosophy of simplicity is embodied to create a smoother execution of tasks, such as modern coffee machines like the Nespresso, extraneous buttons are removed for just two interactable elements: large or small coffee. Two buttons to execute the task. All other mechanisms are hidden, removed, or conjoined with other machine operations to complete tasks, such as opening the reservoir to put in a new coffee capsule resulting in simultaneously discarding the previously used capsule.

DESIGNING INTRIGUE

The element of intrigue plays a vital role in capturing user attention and guiding decision-making. For example, mapping services like Google Maps employ the highlighting of keywords and text similar to a search query. In the example image below, Google extracts relevant information to make the restaurant more interesting and relatable to the user's needs. This approach leverages social proof to spark curiosity, encouraging users to explore businesses based on reviews from other users that mention the terms being queried.

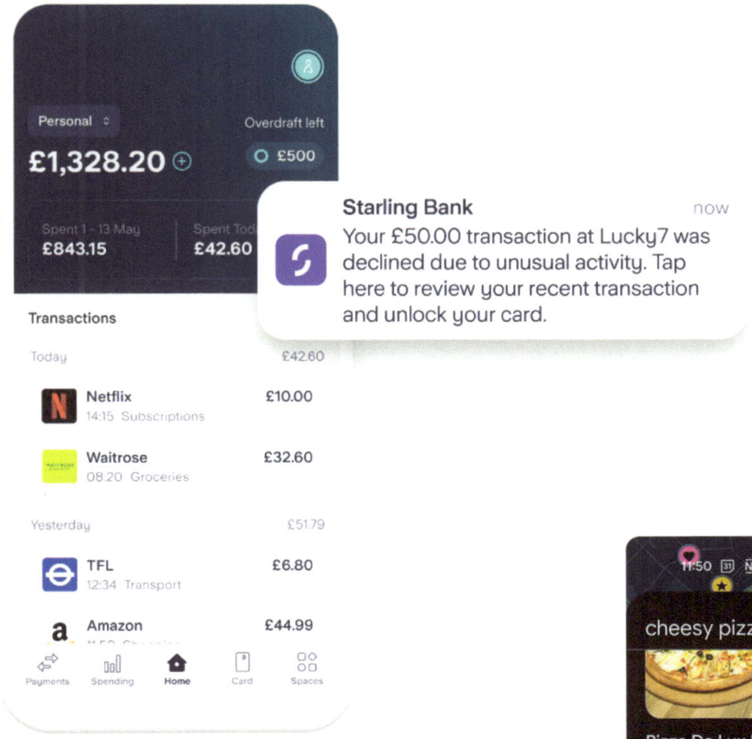

Figure 41: Fraud Detection Marketing Material (Starling Bank)

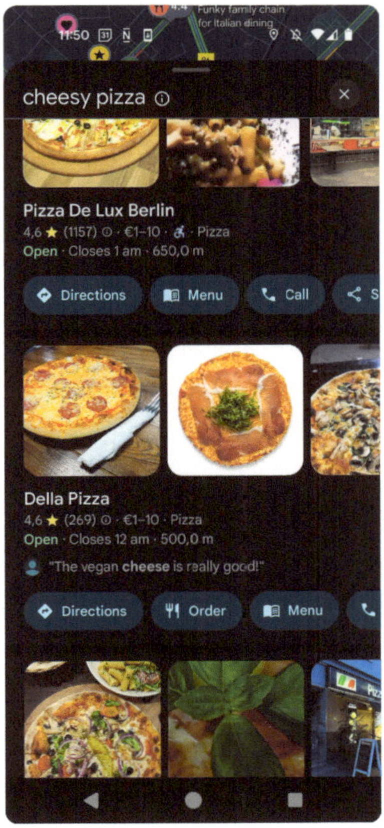

Figure 42: Identifying Keywords to Help mark Relevant Material (Google Maps)

In the financial sector, user interface design elements are often used to draw attention to critical issues like potential fraud. By visually highlighting alerts and notifications, these systems engage users, prompting them to take action. This strategic use of intrigue not only informs users but also empowers them to make informed decisions, thereby enhancing their **sense of agency** in navigating financial transactions.

The design elements of educate, simplify, and intrigue are not merely functional; they reflect deeper trends in our relationship with technology. As machines become more integrated into daily life, their design shapes our interactions with them, influencing how we perceive their roles and capabilities. The educational attribute of ESI fosters a learning relationship between humans and machines, with users continually informed and updated. Simplification reduces technical jargon, helping users to understand AI and ML without the need to be domain experts. Intrigue sparks curiosity and drives exploration.

In exploring these concepts, reflect on the broader implications of evolving interactions with technology. As we increasingly rely on machines for information, communication, and decision-making, the ESI design principles will improve the convoluted nature of intelligent system interactions.

Educate Versus Intrigue

The combination of designing for intrigue and designing for education presents a nuanced challenge. These two facets—interest and education—are critical to crafting digital products that balance user needs and business requirements.

Designing for education entails imparting knowledge and facilitating comprehension of complex systems, particularly in areas such as machine learning where transparency is often obscured by algorithmic complexity, known as the **black box** issue. Educational design clarifies concepts that may be esoteric or counterintuitive to the average user. So, although educational elements do serve a purpose, they also raise a question: "Is an educational component universally requisite across all products?" The answer is contingent on the product's intended function and the user's baseline familiarity with the subject matter.

Think about how consumers understand novel systems like autonomous cars or interact with casual intelligent social media systems like TikTok. Compare this to the relatively simple, better-understood systems with clear mental models like an email spam filter or a smartphone's autocorrect feature.

In domains where technical intricacies are prevalent, such as most ML data-driven applications, educational content is indispensable for demystifying processes and empowering users with a foundational understanding of how the machine operates. Educational attributes of transparent ML design include demonstrating to users how the machine perceives them, their wants and needs.

Conversely, designing for interest is meant to captivate the user's attention and provoke intellectual curiosity. This design paradigm is crucial for creating a basic level of engagement, especially in environments saturated with content and features. Think of products with endless feeds, or numerous buttons and controls. Users need support to navigate these convoluted pathways and interaction options.

Though it can be debated, the inclusion of **intrigue** as a transparent design quality serves to elevate users' trust in ML systems. Building trust by way of bolstering the relationship between system and user. Moving that relationship away from passive consumption toward activation of the user's critical thinking. The challenge lies in striking a balance where the informational content is not only accessible but also compelling enough to foster some level of intrigue from the user.

Imagine the average user is a middle school student, often unaware of how important certain topics are. No matter how much a teacher emphasizes the need to learn something, a student won't pay attention unless there's something intriguing about the lesson. That's why teachers often make learning fun by connecting abstract concepts to real-world examples. For instance, they might explain gravity by discussing why objects fall or how roller coasters work. This approach makes the lesson more engaging and memorable.

While educational content fulfills a utilitarian function to ensure that users are adequately informed, the infusion of intrigue into a design element adds a dimension of appeal, one that can push the user to **notice and learn**. This approach is vital for fostering an environment where users are not only passengers of an intelligent system's decision-making but also active participants in the journey, aligning the machine's values to that of users' needs and their expectations of the machine.

Addressing the black box problem presents a significant challenge. It requires a design strategy combining educational transparency with interesting presentation. By clarifying the pathways of the data flow and decision-making processes, designers can mitigate user alienation felt when interacting with opaque intelligent systems.

ESI "easy"

Users may feel alienated when a system starts to perform actions that seem contrary to their intentions or expectations. For example, a navigation app that suddenly reroutes a user without explaining the reasoning—such as traffic conditions or road closures—can frustrate users and erode trust in the system. Similarly, an intelligent system that provides irrelevant information, such as a voice assistant responding to a specific query about local events with unrelated online search results, can leave users feeling unheard and misunderstood. These examples underscore the importance of creating systems that are not only functional but also intuitive and aligned with users' goals.

The objective is to discern intersecting points of user interest and educational need.

What are the users interested in—and how might a machine deviate from their values? How might the machine manipulate, even unintentionally?

Interest elements can elevate a user's comprehension by gaining their attention, while transparency does not always imply a user's awareness of such transparency. Take for instance a recommendation algorithm on a streaming platform that provides an explanation like, "We recommended this because it's similar to what you've watched." While this is transparent, it might not fully capture the user's attention or enhance their understanding. On the other hand, if the platform includes an interactive element—such as a visual map showing connections between watched content, genres, and user preferences—this can spark curiosity and make the explanation more memorable. By blending transparency with intriguing elements, users gain both awareness and deeper comprehension of the system's functionality.

Viewing, selecting, editing, expanding, and exploring. These are all different levels of engagement. Each offers unique benefits and sacrifices when measured against user task flows. Some interaction methods are quick and superficial, others deep and distracting. Understanding the move from passive consumption to active engagement, then to prolonged exploration—each phase retains a different value to users. Surface value versus deep intellectual questioning of a system's operability and mental models. A baseline measurement of intrigue must be set uniquely with each experience and each product. There is not a one-size-fits-all solution for building transparent AI and ML systems.

THOUGHT EXPERIMENT

Two examples.

- **Example A**: In an e-commerce checkout flow where the platform recommends similar products with the help of ML, an ESI element could harnesses **intrigue** to such an extent that it consistently pushes users away from clicking the "Pay Now" button. The interface design might make use of a small pop-up message with additional information about why a product was recommended (intriguing the user). This message would be so enticing that it consistently distracts users from completing their purchase (for instance, by redirecting them into how the AI makes suggestions). This is inadequate design; it fails its purpose.

  But an element that occasionally (when relevant) draws the user's interest, before selecting "Pay Now", giving them a chance to read the detailed reasonings for why a product was recommended - This would be acceptable. The difference? Though hard to discern, a game of cat and mouse is played to identify the right time and place to display the transparency information being provided. This balance is subtle but critical: users must benefit from the extra knowledge without feeling interrupted. Testing with a large and diverse customer cohort aids in identifying an acceptable solution.

- **Example B**: Online dating apps often include intelligent matching algorithms. Suppose the app includes a feature that occasionally reveals a hidden "compatibility score" between users following several conversations. If implemented thoughtfully, this could add an element of intrigue that deepens the user's engagement without steering them away from organic interactions. However, if the app surfaces this score (or the attributes contributing to it) too frequently or prominently, users might begin to rely on it as a definitive indicator of compatibility, overwhelming their personal impressions and human interactions.

  This could ultimately reduce engagement by creating a dependency on numerical ratings rather than encouraging genuine exploration and human connection. By strategically revealing or withholding such information, the app can keep users curious and invested while preserving a balance between guidance and user autonomy.

To design **simple** is to reduce.

To design **simple** is to adapt - to users - to an environment.

To design **simple** is to listen and observe.

To design **education** is to guide.

To design **education** is to empower.

To design **education** is to be inclusive.

To design **intrigue** is to attract.

To design **intrigue** is to differentiate.

To design **intrigue** is to balance.

V

Visualising ESI

Transparency elements that harness the ESI framework can come in many sizes and shapes, many forms and flavors. Through all the various ways to make transparent the relationship between machine and user, it's most important to test with a wide audience. To assess the usefulness of the information. The content may be more or less useful to different types of users and for each user in different circumstances and real-world scenarios. As for designers, testing should be the cornerstone of your work.

Visualising ESI

To consider the variability of applying the ESI framework, consider the examples explored in this chapter. Designed as a point of inspiration, hopefully, they broaden your perspective regarding ways to apply the design characteristics of **educational**, **simple**, and **intriguing**. These are brought to life in the following examples of various consumer products. Each encompasses many integration methods, large and small in scale.

Important note: The information displayed may not be relevant to all users. The chosen content is merely to showcase a literal method of delivering transparency. Designers will need to test for user feedback within their own projects.

Food Delivery

From left to right:

- **Checkout screen**: Shows food attributes, with two levels of information depth.
- **Search screen**: Color-coded icons can indicate important information about each AI suggested food result, helping users with quick decision-making.
- **Discovery feed**: The highest level of detail, with explainers (notice the difference in the stage of the user journey, checkout versus search versus discovery).

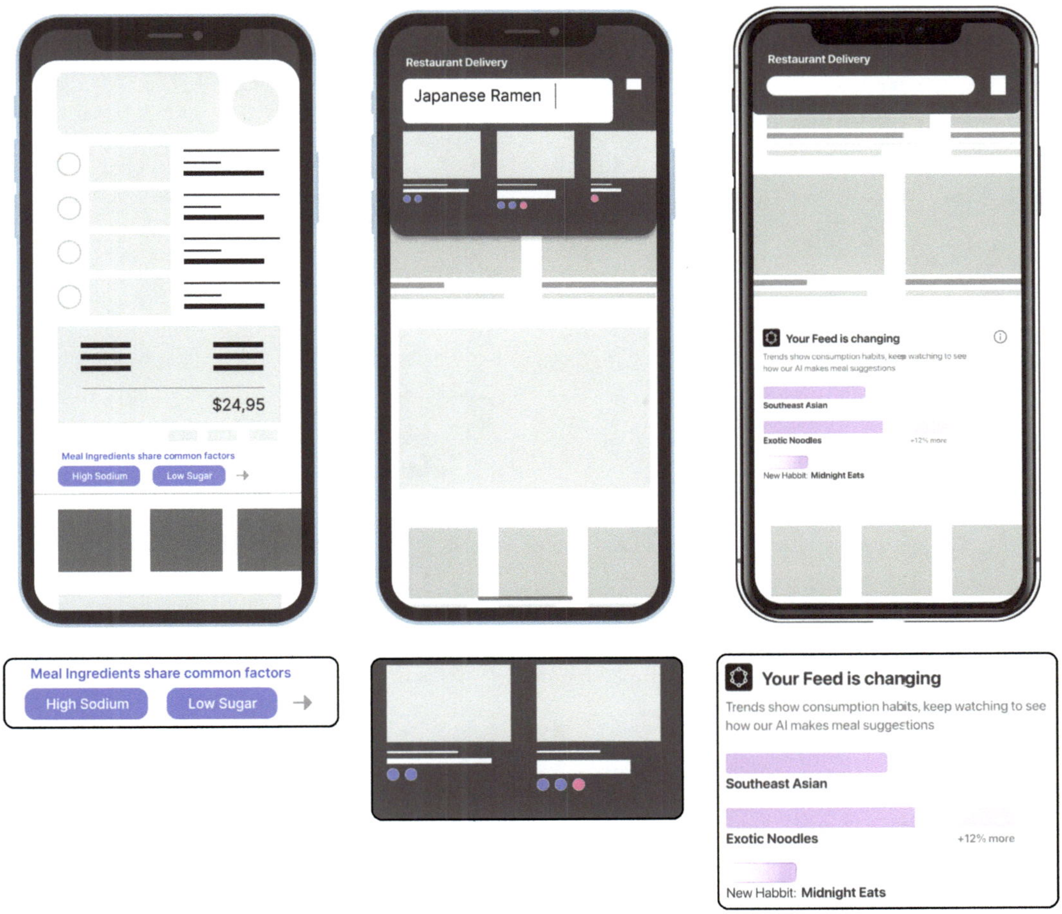

E-commerce

Notice the bottom right-hand corner of the screen, which displays a graphic letting users know how they are developing habits as they interact with the system.

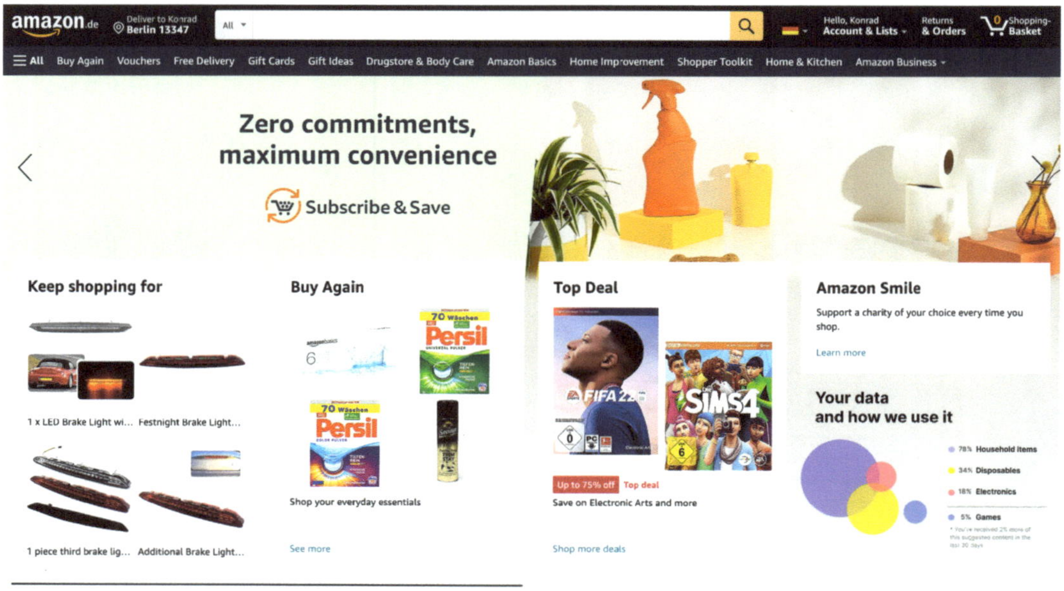

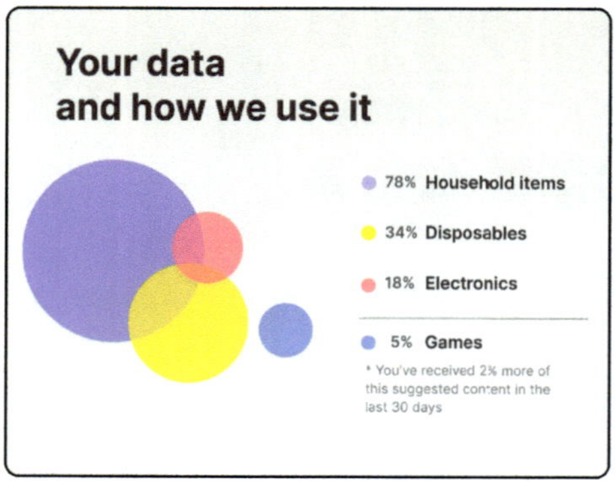

Automotive

Transparent AI for car interfaces, showing information about how the intelligent system senses the current physical attributes of the vehicle and it's environment. Notice how that translates to data unique to the users current situation.

(Tesla Infotainment Example Concept)

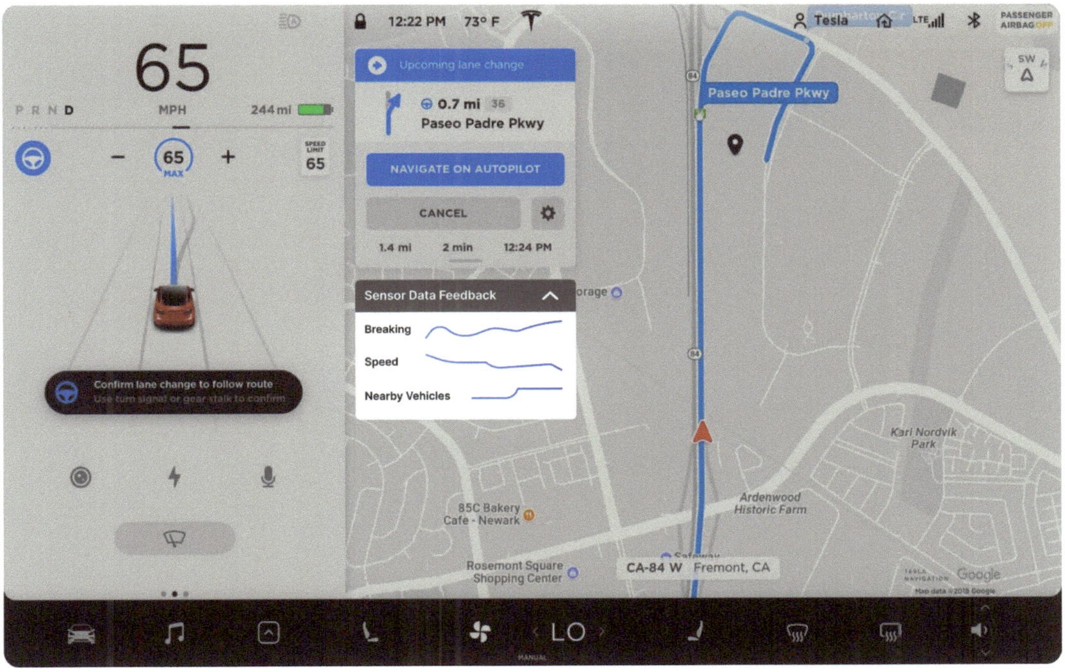

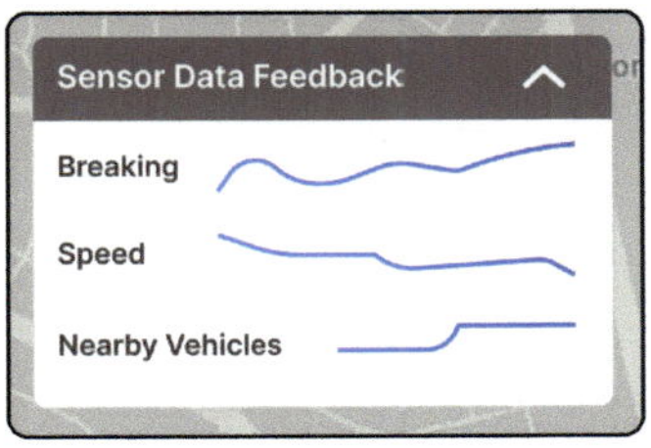

Mail

An email client, with machine learning transparency, helps to make it clear why a message was sent to spam or the similarity of the email to previous ones, giving insight into how mail is automatically filtered.

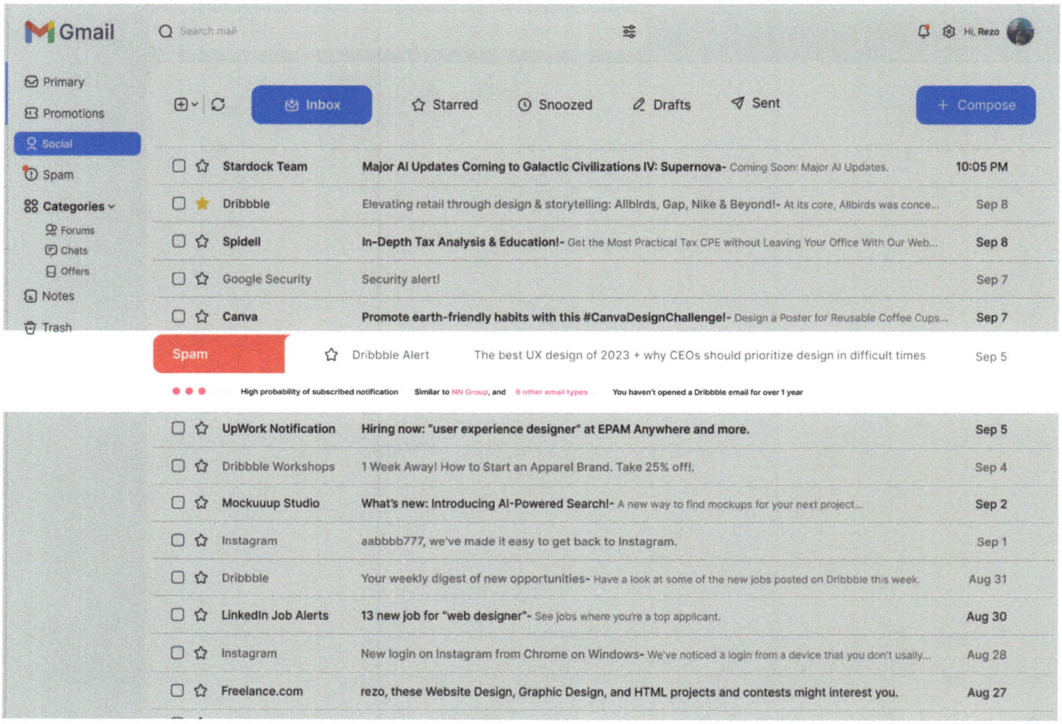

Social

From left to right:

- **Create a story card**: ESI elements showing the connectedness (ML Features) of media content below each card.
- **Notifications feed**: The system might be highlighting certain friends more than others or encouraging conversations with specific connections through choice architecture manipulation. Offering users transparency information does not need to imply highlighting negative interactions.

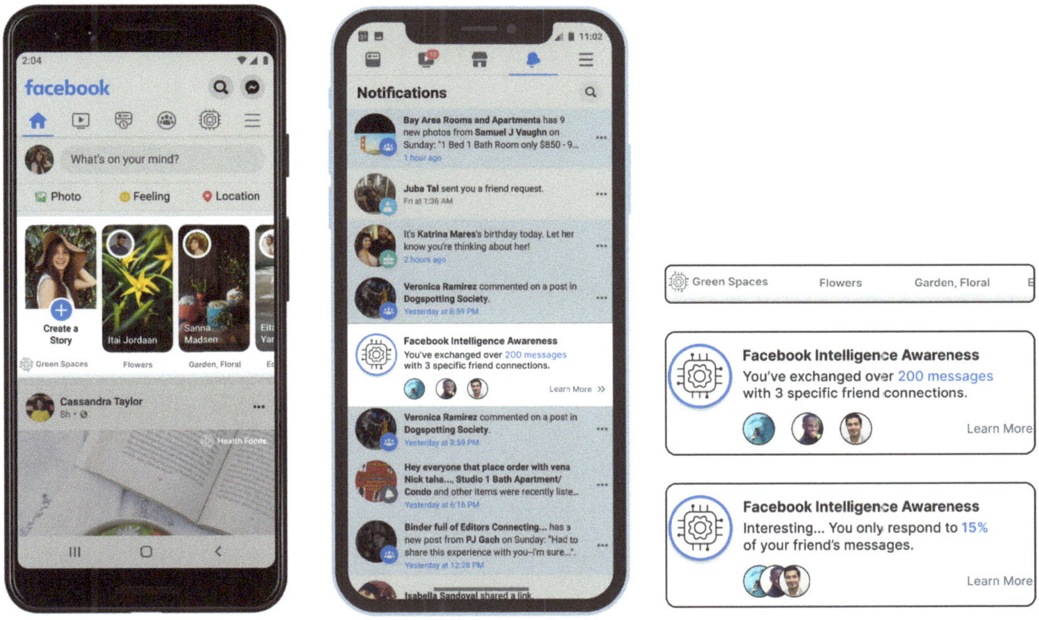

Note: Not all information is necessarily valuable to all users. Careful testing is required to identify which transparency content provides useful information to the highest number of users (e.g., on the left-most screen, the images are correlated from the machine's point of view, which might not be highly relevant or educational to users).

Goals and Limitations

If we design and implement ESI attributes into our products, how do we know if they've been successful?

Classic design methodologies would suggest metrics like the following:

- Engagement with the intelligent system (feature engagement rates).
- User's qualitative perception of attributes (NPS scoring).
- Testing accuracy of user's mental models (e.g., how that AI system works, what is happening when they interact).
- Users' perception of agency for changing the output of the machine.
- Overall product/brand sentiment (TRUST scoring).

These measurements do offer a starting point, though they cannot represent the totality of a user's relationship with a machine. Designed transparency elements using ESI are intended to create a healthier dynamic and understanding of the intelligent system—in both directions.

Whether ML and AI are implemented for finding patterns in data, automation, or content personalization, every implementation increases the amount of variance in a machine's output. What makes ML and AI so powerful is their ability to learn and act rapidly on huge amounts of data, which results in machine operations that can be too hard to monitor or test because of the sheer amount of data and speed of the system's output.

Each user can trigger unique, one-of-a-kind results every time they interact with the system in consumer services. For example, a personalized news aggregator that displays a curated feed based on the user's reading habits. Every feed will look different for every user interacting with that model. Not only what news articles display, but how the articles are headlined or summarized. For less traditional content, variation could include the suggested routes from ML navigation software (e.g., Google Maps), with each user might be presented with slightly different route suggestions.

In the evolving landscape of AI and ML, significant challenges are encountered in discerning and filtering beneficial from harmful content. This issue spans various domains, whether misinformation, filter bubbles, mismatched mental models, or biases. A prominent example is Facebook, which has acknowledged its inability to manage the vast influx of content and the vulgar material that permeates its system (Vincent, 2019). The sheer volume overwhelms human moderators and ML models deployed to mitigate these issues often fail, sometimes exacerbating the spread of abusive content, ultimately sharing content that harms users or silencing users who otherwise should not be.

The crux of the problem lies in the inability of companies to employ enough personnel to effectively monitor platforms and the insufficiency of current ML models to accurately detect and regulate inappropriate content—regardless of how "inappropriate" is defined. This leads us to the question, "What solutions remain viable?"

One promising approach is empowering users with self-monitoring tools, allowing them to control their exposure to certain types of content or autonomous actions taken by machines. Twitter, for instance, explored enabling users to filter content based on their religious beliefs, traditions, and local values, providing a choice to exclude material that they found objectionable (Hern, 2016). This method, while beneficial in shielding users from distressing content, poses significant drawbacks. It risks creating echo chambers where users only encounter information that aligns with their preexisting views, potentially stunting personal growth and awareness by excluding valuable, albeit challenging, perspectives.

In the context of ESI, I advocate for a framework that emphasizes transparency in how user data is processed and interpreted by systems, without imposing judgments on the nature of the content or user behavior. ESI encourages a neutral stance, refraining from dictating what is deemed "good" or "bad" content or machine actions. This approach preserves the user's autonomy to interpret the data and decide their course of action. It respects the inherent subjectivity of defining beneficial or detrimental experiences, acknowledging that these determinations vary widely among individuals.

The core principle of ESI is providing users with comprehensive, clear information about their interactions with digital systems, thereby fostering an informed and conscious user. Transparency is crucial, as it allows users to understand the potential impacts of their data and interactions without prescribing a specific ethical or moral standpoint. The ultimate goal is not to guide users towards a predetermined "better" outcome but to empower them to make informed decisions based on an unbiased presentation of data.

A careful design of interface elements informs without influencing, guides without directing.

Visualising ESI

The future of user experience design in AI and ML must navigate this delicate balance, striving to uphold user autonomy while ensuring a safe and enriching digital environment.

Central to the ESI framework is the notion that users should have the freedom to navigate their digital experiences with a clear understanding of how their data is used and what implications it may have. **It's not only about what data is being used; it is more about the effect that data is having on all the parties involved, both the machine and the user.**

Such transparency is not just a technical feature but a functional UX imperative. Users empowered with knowledge about the systems they interact with are better equipped to make decisions that align with their values and needs—and thus building trust between user and system. This concept extends beyond merely providing opt-out options or content filters; it encompasses a holistic approach where users are educated about the workings of AI models, the nature of data processing, and the potential biases that may influence the content they're exposed to.

Figure 43: Lane-Change Assist (Blind spot markers.)

With so many variables going into a model's computations, it can be hard to discern what the machine is doing with those different inputs, the weights it attaches to them, and how all the different data affects the system's calculations—and ultimately its executive function.

Displaying some of the variables that influence these decisions can be helpful, especially in cases where transparency enhances trust. For instance, a streaming service might tell a user, "We think you'll like this movie because it has a mix of action and romantic comedy, similar to what you enjoyed yesterday." This approach can demystify the recommendation process without overwhelming the user. However, selectively showing variables can sometimes oversimplify the model, making it appear less intelligent or even unsettling.

Imagine if your car informed you it was rerouting a journey because it detected subtle fidgeting and assumed you needed a bathroom break. That level of monitoring would likely feel invasive, causing discomfort rather than convenience. Another example could be a fitness app notifying a user that "We've reduced your running goal this week because you skipped yesterday's workout." While this explanation aims for clarity, it might make the app seem overly simplistic or judgmental, as if it's ignoring other possible factors like injury recovery or a busy schedule. This level of narrow reasoning could make the app feel less thoughtful or even intrusive.

The ultimate value of ESI comes from providing users with information on the effects of their interaction with the machine, not only the data itself—what is collected and why it is collected.

Suppose a smart driving assistant uses eye-tracking technology to monitor driver alertness. Instead of informing the user that it's scanning their eyes every few milliseconds to detect signs of fatigue—a detail that might feel invasive and raise privacy concerns—the system could provide actionable insights based on the effects of detected fatigue. For instance, if signs of drowsiness were detected, the system might display a friendly suggestion on the dashboard, such as "Consider taking a short break soon—refreshing can make your drive safer and more enjoyable." This approach maintains transparency without disclosing every technical detail, focusing instead on the benefit to the user. Or perhaps instead of text, there was a simple visual cue that blinked rapidly, altering the user to pull over and refresh, similarly to how modern cars now have blind spot lane-change assist.

*FOOTNOTE: Weight is a numerical parameter that determines the strength of the connection between input features and the output in a model. Weights are adjusted during training to minimize errors and improve the model's performance.

Visualising ESI

Figure 44: Ford Edsel

A productivity app that monitors user activity to provide focus-enhancing tips, the system could go beyond merely telling users it's tracking their "typing speed" or "click frequency." Instead, it could share insights on the effects of productivity patterns like: "You seem to be more focused during the morning hours—would you like a reminder to tackle high-priority tasks then?" By presenting data in this way, the app adds value through insights that feel natural and personalized, without highlighting every specific variable it's monitoring. Once again, these transparency elements don't need to require displaying information on a screen. Perhaps the productivity app is linked to your smartwatch and vibrates constantly in times of poor productivity performance. Invasive or helpful?

Though it may already be obvious, there is no easy answer or perfect solution for improving the relationship between users and intelligent machines. Both self-monitoring on behalf of the user is required and a minimum standard for system transparency that allows users to understand how the system is working and its dynamics of influence. The challenge lies in defining what constitutes harmful content/actions in a manner that is culturally sensitive, legally compliant, and aligned with community standards.

The Dark Side of Transparency

When Henry Ford, the maker of the infamous Model T, set forth to disrupt the automotive industry, he had many goals in mind, including optimizing workflow, producing more vehicles with less effort, and creating an economic empire that would span decades. In many ways, Ford got his wish. The brand name still exists today, albeit with some product launches that could have gone smoother. There were many successes and failures. The Model T was the first mass-production vehicle.

The Ford Mustang, the first pony car, went on to define a new class of American muscle cars. The Ford Pinto was famous for its controversial safety flaws and fire hazards. And then there's the story of the Ford Edsel.

The Edsel is not only a story of a company's ineptness in reading consumer and market needs but also a humbling experience regarding what transparency can do to an organization and a product campaign.

Ford spent years transparently conducting extensive market research before launching the Edsel, a new line of automobiles designed to be the perfect car based on consumer preferences. They promoted its development using public input, claiming that they were listening to their customers, which was innovative compared to other manufacturers that kept their cards closer to the chest. The Ford Edsel was going to be a car for the people, by the people (Chi, 2021).

However, when it was finally released the public reaction was negative. The car was overengineered due to conflicting consumer feedback; its pricing and marketing felt artificial rather than exciting. Consumers began to doubt Ford's ability to understand what they actually wanted, leading to one of the most infamous product failures in history. Instead of building trust, Ford's overemphasis on developmental transparency led to skepticism and disappointment.

Similarly, the upstart Tesla also struggled with transparency. In an effort to roll out and gain adoption and usage of Telsa's Full Self-Driving (FSD) technology, the company included real-time updates and full access to the companies beta-software to gain public support for usage. (Remember, training data from consumers was critical for slowly building an AI system that could handle all the random occurrences that can happen on the road. In this instance, more data = better system performance.) Unfortunately, this fueled both excitement and controversy. While the company aimed to keep users informed and usage of the software high, this openness led some drivers to overestimate FSD's capabilities, mistakenly believing it could handle all driving conditions without human intervention. This misunderstanding has resulted in multiple accidents, including fatal crashes. Tesla's FSD case is an example of irresponsible communication as well as a disregard for restricting access to features not yet ready for live environments. Transparency can be problematic from both a marketing and disclosure perspective. Limiting users' access to early software releases can be advantageous (e.g., FSD beta program updates).

Regulators have taken notice. The National Highway Traffic Safety Administration (NHTSA) launched an investigation into 2.4 million Tesla vehicles after reports of collisions involving FSD. The probe focused on whether Tesla's messaging contributed to driver misuse. Additionally, in 2022, Tesla faced a class-action lawsuit alleging that the company misled consumers about its self-driving technology, portraying it as more advanced than it truly was (Mann, 2024).

Tesla's transparency, meant to build trust and showcase progress, instead sparked safety concerns, legal challenges, and regulatory scrutiny—highlighting how fraught the battle can be between innovation and responsible communication.

A more whimsical transparency scandal was McDonald's pink-slime disaster. In response to public concerns over the use of "pink slime"—a meat byproduct treated with ammonium hydroxide—in its products, McDonald's released videos detailing its food preparation processes to assure customers of its quality. The outcome? Their transparency efforts backfired as they inadvertently reminded consumers of the controversy, leading to increased public scrutiny and a temporary decline in sales. McDonald's story of good intentions gone wrong parallels the risks tech companies face when pressured by passionate ethics advocates to disclose how their AI and ML models make decisions. If businesses lean too far into transparency—revealing how they adjust intelligent consumer systems to favor positive-growth metrics—it can become a dangerous strategy (Wikipedia, n.d.-b).

Transparency is such a double-edged sword. Cutting from both sides and causing havoc when improperly deployed. It requires a careful balance of understanding user sentiment, user domain expertise, and internal/external business risks. These different opposing factors can only be reconciled if designers and engineers work together to craft digital experiences that build comprehension of systems, therefore increasing trust, yet withholding mission/system critical IP that could be used to harm the company.

When Trust Fails

The promise of artificial intelligence in commercial applications is, at its core, a seductive one: the elimination of inefficiency, the erasure of friction, and the orchestration of seamless interactions between consumer and system. The logic of this implementation appears unimpeachable. Why burden individuals with cumbersome decision-making processes when algorithmic intelligence can synthesize vast quantities of data to present them with precisely what they need—often before they even realize they need it? AI, when deployed in financial services, retail, and countless other domains, is idealized on this fundamental premise: by reducing cognitive load, optimizing choices, and engineering convenience it enhances both the user experience and corporate profitability.

The very mechanism that makes such systems appear frictionless is also the source of their inherent fragility. Their function hinges not merely on technical precision but on a more elusive and intangible variable: trust. Unlike the mechanistic operations of a vending machine or an ATM, which execute predetermined commands without interpretation, AI and ML-infused systems exist in a liminal space. Part deterministic, part probabilistic. They do not simply retrieve; they infer. They do not merely display; they predict. They cease the offering of repetitive product experiences and instead deliver a unique individual experience to each user. In doing so, they require an implicit contract of confidence from the user, a willingness to believe that the invisible processes shaping their experience are both benign and equitable. An erosion of this trust, once initiated, has a cascading effect—one that is particularly stark in cases where the AI system is tasked with decision-making in deeply personal or high-stakes domains.

Consider the case of Apple Card's AI-driven credit allocation. The apparent innovation was clear: unlike traditional underwriting processes, which relied on cloudy human judgment, AI could evaluate creditworthiness in a manner that was both instantaneous and unbiased. By analyzing financial patterns, spending behaviors, and credit histories, it could offer credit limits dynamically and equitably, stripping away the inefficiencies of

human subjectivity. The intended benefit was dual-faceted. The consumer, freed from the delays and inconsistencies of traditional financial gatekeeping, would experience greater accessibility to credit, while Apple and its banking partner, Goldman Sachs, could streamline operations and mitigate risk through algorithmic precision (Mills, 2019).

Visualising ESI

This utopian vision of a purely rationalized credit system collapsed when discrepancies emerged, most notably in the case of high-profile applicants like David Heinemeier Hansson, whose wife, despite sharing identical financial circumstances, received a credit limit 20 times lower than his own. The outcry that followed was not simply a reaction to one anomalous case of financial inequality but an existential reckoning with the unseen forces governing algorithmic decision-making. If AI was indeed impartial, why did it so closely mirror the same biases and exclusions that had long characterized human-led financial institutions? If it was truly a mechanism of fairness, why could neither Apple nor Goldman Sachs provide a coherent explanation for the discrepancies?

Figure 45: Apple Card

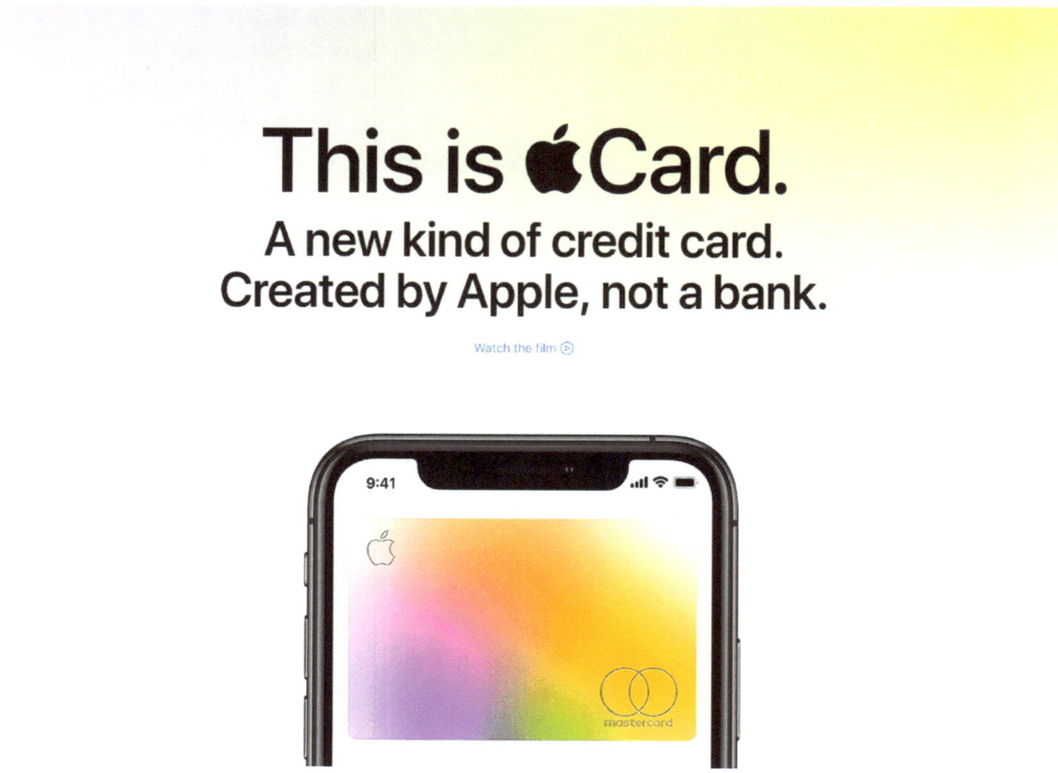

The philosophical implications of such failures are profound. AI, in theory, is designed to function as an arbiter of efficiency, yet when its workings are impossible to interpret, it takes on the characteristics of an unaccountable authority—one that dictates access to resources, not through comprehensible logic but through mechanisms that resist questioning. The psychological effect on the user is one of alienation. A system that was meant to be an enabler instead becomes an unexplainable gatekeeper, one that appears to operate by principles that remain obscured. The moment this opacity is recognized, the user reevaluates their willingness to engage. The fundamental assumption of AI—that it exists as an aid rather than an impediment—begins to erode. Trust, once fractured, is often hard to restore to its original value.

A parallel can be drawn to Amazon's personalization algorithms, another case in which the initial promise of AI devolved into a framework of manipulation and mistrust. Amazon, in its early iterations, hoped to be seen as a relatively neutral platform—a digital storefront where users navigated through static categories of products. Search results were governed by direct user input; recommendations, while rudimentary, did not interfere with the basic mechanics of choice. The introduction of AI-driven personalization transformed this landscape, purportedly for the better. The algorithmic architecture behind Amazon's recommendation engine was designed to surface relevant products with unprecedented precision, creating a system that would intuit consumer desires before they were consciously articulated. In its idealized form, this would reduce decision fatigue, streamline purchasing, and drive higher engagement.

Yet, as with Apple Card's AI underwriting, this system began to display unintended consequences that called into question its underlying legitimacy. The first tremors of distrust surfaced when consumers began noticing price fluctuations not driven by supply and demand but by AI's ability to segment and exploit a user's willingness to pay. The realization that two users, engaging with the same product page, could be presented with starkly different pricing structures based on the system's assessment of their purchasing habits introduced a troubling paradigm: the algorithm was no longer merely optimizing their experience, it was strategically shaping their behavior in ways they could not easily perceive.

The final rupture occurred when reports emerged of Amazon's own products being systematically elevated in search rankings, even when competing products held superior reviews or lower prices. What had once been a seemingly neutral marketplace had been transformed into an ecosystem in which AI, rather than facilitating choice, was exerting control over it. The psychological impact on users was interesting. The system's recommendations, once regarded as an aid, began to be viewed as an act of coercion. The more AI attempted to anticipate desires, the more users felt manipulated, which resulted not just in dissatisfaction but a withdrawal of engagement. The consumer, having lost faith in the integrity of the system, responded by resisting it.

Most famous were incidents of ridiculously priced goods, like Peter Lawrence's *The Making of a Fly*, in which the price of a book was driven upwards in ridiculous fashion until it hit $23,698,655.93 (Solon, 2011).

Another trust-breaking example is the 2014 Lindt Café siege, a hostage situation that unfolded in Sydney, Australia. Uber's AI-driven ride-sharing app noticed an uptick in demand during the crisis and acted autonomously. Its surge pricing algorithm was triggered, causing fares to quadruple as people desperately tried to flee the area; some customers reported being charged over $100 for very short rides. After major backlash, Uber quickly reversed course and offered refunds, as well as free rides out of the danger zone.

This case is a prime example of the possible negative effects of machine learning and automated systems.

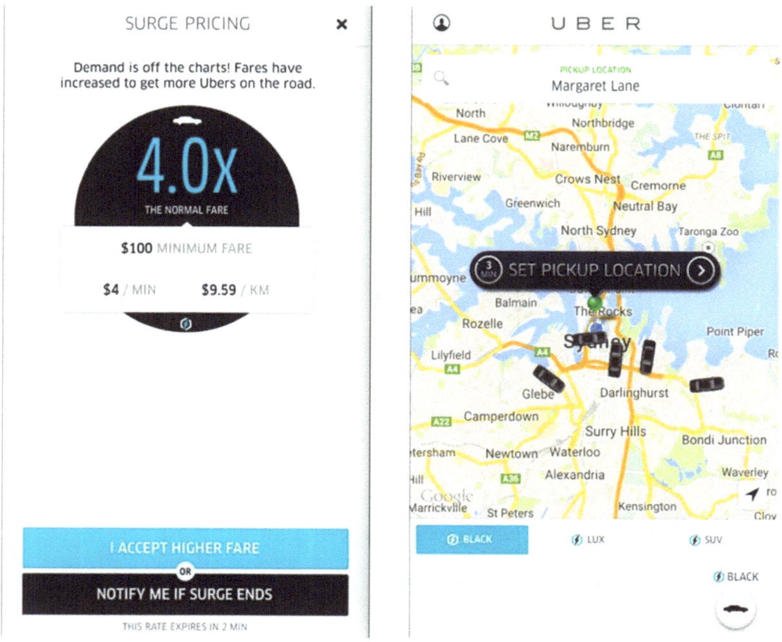

Figure 46: Uber Surge Pricing

While theoretically beneficial in balancing supply and demand, they can lead to questionable business practices, tarring a brand's image. The effects of that "crisis moment" could not be rewound (Cresci, 2014).

What unites these cases is that businesses that hope to profit from AI will have the most to lose when user trust is mismanaged. As consumers' awareness and knowledge of intelligent systems naturally increases over time (similar to how smartphone adoption spread with technological literacy), they develop a deeper understanding of how these systems work. This evolution suggests that users will undoubtedly become more inspective of AI- and ML-enabled systems. The result is a consumer base that grows increasingly critical of intelligent system behavior, actively seeking evidence of whether such systems truly serve their needs and values.

The broader philosophical question emerging from these failures is whether AI can ever truly function as an unbiased facilitator of human decision-making or whether it is, by its very nature, an extension of the power structures that create and deploy it. If AI reflects the values embedded in its training data, does it not simply reproduce the inequities it was meant to resolve? And if AI is ultimately engineered to optimize corporate interests, can it ever align itself with users in a way that does not eventually lead to their exploitation?

These failures do not simply represent technical shortcomings; they signal a deeper reckoning with the nature of algorithmic authority. For AI to be widely accepted, it must not only be functional but also perceived as trustworthy. The systems that succeed in the long-term will not merely be those that are the most efficient, or profitable, but those that embed transparency and accountability at their core—in ways benefiting both user and business. Without these elements, AI ceases to function as an enabler of human agency and instead becomes a mechanism of unseen coercion—a development that users, inevitably, will reject.

Closing Thoughts

In 20 years, what will it mean to be human? How will we know our actions and thoughts are truly ours, uniquely originating from our desires? Will we be certain that we still maintain agency over our worldviews and perceptions that define our individualism?

In 20 years, how much of our work will be done by machines? Regardless of the scale of those actions, or how visibly they are perceived. Aware of the accelerating pace of decision-making, enabled by intelligent agents—whether through reinforcement learning in recommendation systems, or actions taken entirely autonomously by machines designed to automate our lives (e.g., driverless cars, smart thermostats, jail-time judgments, and loan approvals). For is this not the goal? To increase the speed, efficiency, and effectiveness of decision-making. Learning and Doing.

If the way we write emails, make coffee, drive to the park, read the news, shop for clothes, educate children, apply to jobs, and identify cancers are all beholden to the power of machine learning, what do we gain, what do we lose? Even if we exclude high-risk sectors like finance or health care, do these machine -influencing factors not multiply and result in a human that is now somewhat inhuman? Are we still 100% human?

This is not to be confused with a total loss of human autonomy. No, instead it is the delta at which theorists describe the point in human history where machines and humans connect so deeply that the ratio of human versus machine decisions is no longer perceptible. We have yet to give a name to this moment in human history.

I assume that in writing this book I may have missed particular research and contradicted majority opinion on certain matters. Or that readers may outright feel put off and agitated by the stances taken. Though these may be the outcome and results, I can only hope the reader comes away with a more holistic approach to understanding intelligent machines and the implications of UX on machine learning technologies.

In my research and writing the purpose was to learn about the subject of machine learning to better articulate how traditional UX design has been upset by the implications of large-scale ML, particularly within consumer applications.

Over the next 25 years, the titles given to today's technologies will surely change (LLM, ML, Deep Learning, GPTs, agentic design, etc.). Methods of application will also evolve. What will not change is the underlying effects of machine learning, and its ability to empower faster learning, identification, and task completion. But this same technology will also empower manipulative intents and generate issues relating to discreet influence.

Influence and manipulation can be beneficial and useful. They can also be used to harm individuals.

It is my belief that design and engineering must adapt their approach to creating transparency solutions, to counter the negative side effects of these systems, and to bolster the positive outcomes from our new technologies.

* * *

This book, and the concepts within it, are not meant to be a criticism of what came before. It is to the forefathers of design that we must show our thanks, as they have led us to where we are today.

This book also does not provide all the necessary answers to the problems that IIS brings. Nor do I hope to counter all the side effects that machine learning has on human operators. The ideas shared are meant to be a continuum of what was before and what lies ahead. It is an outline for a good structure on which to design intelligent machines. This is not the be-all and end-all fix for things that may evolve in the future. Instead, it serves as ground-level research of my era and what I've encountered during my short but exhaustive career in software technologies.

Appendix

Adapted from "Explainable Artificial Intelligence (XAI): Concepts, Taxonomies, Opportunities and Challenges toward Responsible AI" by Alejandro Barredo Arrieta and colleagues (2019).

*List is truncated and recomposed for clarity, and applicability to ESI.

- **Trustworthiness:** Will the machine or program act as it's intended when faced with a problem? A good thing to note is not every trustworthy system is considered explainable. This is to mean users might trust the system, but not be able to articulate why or point to specific system actions/logic which explains why they have that trust.

- **Causality:** Inference about the relationships between different observable data points—how is the data related, what caused what.

- **Transferability:** Understanding the relationships taking place in the data can help users reuse this existing structure and knowledge in future use cases (if the system worked "this way" in the past, it might work a similar way for a similar problem in the future). Note that not every transferable model should be considered explainable.

- **Informativeness:** As machine learning is ultimately there to help make decisions faster. The problem being solved by the machine should not be confused with the problem the user sets out to solve. The informativeness goal is to help draw distinctions and clarification, keeping a user from conflating the answer of the machine (output) with the answer to the problem that the user seeks. These can be different.

- **Confidence:** This criterion helps to indicate the robustness and stability of the system. Confidence can only be truly associated with machine learning models that are considered reliable. In the case of our interpretations of XAI, reliable systems are ones that have a high level of confidence by the same party. They go hand in hand.

- **Fairness:** Ethical considerations of the model. Based on the output of the system, from a social standpoint, how fair does the model seem to be?

Appendix

- **Accessibility:** This goal focuses on a model's ability to be understood by non-technical people. This is a primary goal of ESI and one of the most important elements of what makes a model successful from a design perspective (for consumers). A large portion of the text in the book focuses on how to solve this.

  NOTE: Accessibility does not denote an AI system's ability to be comprehended by a user. In Barredo Arrieta and colleagues' definition, we must draw a distinction as it's a two-part problem. A user's ability to see and access the AI system's operational methods (displaying how the system is making decisions) and how a user can comprehend the information or actions produced by the machine. We can refer to this as accessibility versus comprehension.

- **Interactivity:** What ability are users given to tweak the model to ensure optimal performance and preferred output?

- **Privacy:** As it relates to the goal mentioned by Barredo Arrieta and colleagues means an ability to explain how a model is connected to the user's data and the relations of their data and that model, by unauthorized third parties. Not being able to understand what data has been captured by the model and used to perform its functions might entail privacy issues. Where did the data originate from, how is that data interpreted, and how that data is applied within the inner constructs of the model can relate to privacy in systems where the collected data is sensitive or ambiguous.

Reference List

Abstrabit Technologies. 2024. "Unleashing AI's Next Evolution: From Cognitive Systems to Action-Oriented Agents." LinkedIn, December 25. https://www.linkedin.com/pulse/unleashing-ais-next-evolution-from-cognitive-systems-action-oriented-khpzc/.

Amershi, Saleema, Dan Weld, Mihaela Vorvoreanu, et al. 2019. "Guidelines for Human-AI Interaction" in *Proceedings of the 2019 CHI Conference on Human Factors in Computing Systems*, 1–13. https://doi.org/10.1145/3290605.3300233.

Baker, Dylan. 2022. "Datasets Have Worldviews." PAIR. https://pair.withgoogle.com/explorables/dataset-worldviews/.

Barredo Arrieta, Alejandro, Natalia Díaz-Rodríguez, Javier Del Ser, and Adrien Bennetot. 2019. "Explainable Artificial Intelligence (XAI): Concepts, Taxonomies, Opportunities and Challenges toward Responsible AI." *Information Fusion 58*, no. 3. DOI:10.1016/j.inffus.2019.12.012.

Bellotti, Victoria, and Keith Edwards. 2004. "Intelligibility and Accountability: Human Considerations in Context Aware Systems." *Human-Computer Interaction 16*. 10.1207/S15327051HCI16234_05.

Binns, Reuben, et al. 2018. "'It's Reducing a Human Being to a Percentage': Perceptions of Justice in Algorithmic Decisions" in *Proceedings of the 2018 CHI Conference on Human Factors in Computing Systems*, 1–14. https://doi.org/10.1145/3173574.3173951.

Bishop, John Mark. 2020. "Artificial Intelligence is Stupid and Causal Reasoning Wil Not Fix It." *Frontiers in Psychology 11*, no. 513474. https://www.frontiersin.org/articles/10.3389/fpsyg.2020.513474/full.

Bolukbasi, Tolga, Kai-Wei Chang, James Zou, Venkatesh Saligrama, and Adam Kalai. 2016. "Man Is to Computer Programmer as Woman Is to Homemaker? Debiasing Word Embeddings" in *Proceedings of the 30th International Conference on Neural Information Processing Systems*, 4356–64.

Bunt, Andrea, Matthew Lount, and Catherine Lauzon. 2012. "Are Explanations Always Important? A Study of Deployed, Low-Cost Intelligent Interactive Systems" in *Proceedings of the 2012 ACM International Conference on Intelligent User Interfaces*, 169–178.

Buolamwini, Joy, and Timnit Gebru. 2018. "Gender Shades: Intersectional Accuracy Disparities in Commercial Gender Classification" in *Conference on Fairness, Accountability and Transparency, FAT 2018*, 23–24.

Reference List

Carroll, Micah, Dylan Hadfield-Menell, Stuart Russell, and Anca Dragan. 2021. "Estimating and Penalizing Preference Shift in Recommender Systems" in *RecSys '21: Proceedings of the 15th ACM Conference on Recommender Systems*, 661–67. https://doi.org/10.1145/3460231.3478849

Chi. 2021. "Why the Ford Edsel Product Launch Failed and What Can We Learn from It?" Good Marketing Club, May 30. https://www.goodmarketing.club/marketing-example/why-the-ford-edsel-product-launch-failed-and-what-can-we-learn-from-it.

Chouldechova, Alexandra. 2017. "Fair Prediction with Disparate Impact: A Study of Bias in Recidivism Prediction Instruments." *Big Data* 5, no. 2. https://doi.org/10.1089/big.2016.0047.

Cresci, Elena. 2014. "Uber Offers Free Rides after Backlash over Surge Pricing During Sydney Siege." *Guardian*, December 15. https://www.theguardian.com/technology/2014/dec/15/uber-offers-free-rides-after-backlash-over-surge-pricing-during-sydney-siege.

Culkin, John. 1967. "A Schoolman's Guide to Marshall McLuhan." *The Saturday Review*, March 18, 51–53.

Davies, Dan. 2025. *The Unaccountability Machine: Why Big Systems Make Terrible Decisions—and How the World Lost Its Mind*. University of Chicago Press.

Decision Lab. n.d. "Choice Architecture." Accessed April 11, 2025. https://thedecisionlab.com/reference-guide/psychology/choice-architecture.

Deshpande, Ameet, Tanmay Rajpurohit, Karthik Narasimhan, and Ashwin Kalyan. 2023. "Anthropomorphization of AI: Opportunities and Risks" in *Proceedings of the Natural Legal Language Processing Workshop 2023*, 1–7.

Dourish, Paul. 1997. "Accounting for System Behaviour: Representation, Reflection and Resourceful Action" in *Proceedings of Computers in Context '95*. https://www.academia.edu/2430419/Accounting_for_System_Behaviour_Representation_Reflection_and_Resourceful_Action.

Eliot, Lance. 2020. "On the Beguiling Question of Whether AI Can Form Intent, Including the Case of Self-Driving Cars." *Forbes*, June 6. https://www.forbes.com/sites/lanceeliot/2020/06/06/on-the-beguiling-question-of-whether-ai-can-form-intent-including-the-case-of-self-driving-cars/.

Eren, S. 2024. “Toyota Kata as a Scaffolding for Human-Centric Manufacturing: Applying Lean Thinking for a Digital and Sustainable Factory of the Future” in *Flexible Automation and Intelligent Manufacturing: Establishing Bridges for More Sustainable Manufacturing Systems*, edited by F. J. G. Silva et al. Springer. https://doi.org/10.1007/978-3-031-38165-2_45.

Farquhar, Sebastian, Ryan Carey, and Tom Everitt. 2022. “Path-Specific Objectives for Safer Agent Incentives.” *Proceedings of the AAAI Conference on Artificial Intelligence 36*, no. 9: 9529–38. https://doi.org/10.1609/aaai.v36i9.21186.

Faverio, Michelle. 2023. “Key Findings About Americans and Data Privacy.” Pew Research Center, October 18. https://www.pewresearch.org/short-reads/2023/10/18/key-findings-about-americans-and-data-privacy/.

Gerhardt-Powals, J. 1996. “Cognitive Engineering Principles for Enhancing Human-Computer Performance.” *International Journal of Human-Computer Interaction 8*, no. 2: 189–211. https://doi.org/10.1080/10447319609526147.

Gregoire, Courtney, Iain Drennan, Cathy Li, and Minos Bantourakis. 2023. “Global Principles on Digital Safety: Translating International Human Rights for the Digital Context.” World Economic Forum. https://www3.weforum.org/docs/WEF_Global_Charter_of_Principles_for_Digital_Safety_2023.pdf.

Gunning, David. 2017. “Explainable Artificial Intelligence (XAI).” DARPA/I2O. https://www.darpa.mil/attachments/XAIProgramUpdate.pdf.

Harris, Tristan. 2016. “How Technology Hijacks People’s Minds.” Medium, May 18. medium.com/thrive-global/how-technology-hijacks-peoples-minds-from-a-magician-and-google-s-design-ethicist-56d62ef5edf3.

Hern, Alex. 2016. “Twitter Users to Get Ability to Mute Words and Conversations.” *Guardian*, November 15. https://www.theguardian.com/technology/2016/nov/15/twitter-users-to-get-ability-to-mute-words-and-conversations?utm_source=chatgpt.com.

Hick, W. E. 1952. “On the Rate of Gain of Information.” *Quarterly Journal of Experimental Psychology 4*, no. 1: 11–26. https://doi.org/10.1080/17470215208416600.

Holbrook, Jess, and Josh Lovejoy. 2017. “Human-Centered Machine Learning.” Medium, July 9. https://medium.com/google-design/human-centered-machine-learning-a770d10562cd.

Reference List

Holzinger, Andreas. 2016. "Interactive Machine Learning for Health Informatics: When Do We Need the Human-in-the-Loop?" *Brain Informatics 3*, no. 2: 119–131. doi:10.1007/s40708-016-0042-6.

IBM. 2022. "What Is Human-Centered AI?" March 31. https://research.ibm.com/blog/what-is-human-centered-ai.

Institute of Electrical and Electronics Engineers. 2017. *Aligned Design: A Vision for Prioritizing Human Well-being with Autonomous and Intelligent Systems*, Ver. 2. https://standards.ieee.org/wp-content/uploads/import/documents/other/ead_v2.pdf.

Kästner, Christian. 2022. "Transparency and Accountability in ML-Enabled Systems." Medium, January 10. https://ckaestne.medium.com/transparency-and-accountability-in-ml-enabled-systems-f8ed0b6fd183.

Krakovna, Victoria, et al. 2020. "Specification Gaming: The Flip Side of AI Ingenuity." Google DeepMind, April 21. https://deepmind.google/discover/blog/specification-gaming-the-flip-side-of-ai-ingenuity/.

La Daga, Fabio, and Andrea Bonarini. 1998. "Behavioral Control Architecture with Motivational Approach for Autonomous Agents." Politecnico di Milano, Dipartimento di Elettronica e Informazione.

Lauer, D. 2021. "Facebook's Ethical Failures Are Not Accidental: They Are Part of the Business Model." *AI Ethics 1*: 395–403. https://doi.org/10.1007/s43681-021-00068-x.

Lim, Brian Y., and Anind K. Dey. 2009. "Assessing Demand for Intelligibility in Context-Aware Applications" in *UbiComp '09: Proceedings of the 11th International Conference on Ubiquitous Computing*, 195–204. https://doi.org/10.1145/1620545.1620576.

LinkedIn. n.d. "How Can AI Models Be More Transparent and Explainable When Analyzing Big Data?" Accessed April 11, 2025. https://www.linkedin.com/advice/0/how-can-ai-models-more-transparent-explainable-i0wmf.

Mann, Jyoti. 2024. "Tesla Faces a Fresh Probe from Auto Regulators over Its Full Self-Driving Software." *Business Insider*, October 18. https://www.businessinsider.com/tesla-faces-fresh-probe-from-safety-watchdog-into-fsd-tech-2024-10.

Reference List

Mayer, Anne-Sophie, Franz Strich, and Marina Fiedler. 2020. "Unintended Consequences of Introducing AI Systems for Decision Making." *MIS Quarterly Executive 19*, no. 4. https://aisel.aisnet.org/misqe/vol19/iss4/6.

Mills, Karen. 2019. "Gender Bias Complaints against Apple Card Signal a Dark Side to Fintech." Harvard Business School, November 19. https://www.library.hbs.edu/working-knowledge/gender-bias-complaints-against-apple-card-signal-a-dark-side-to-fintech.

Mollerup, Per. 2015. *Simplicity: A Matter of Design*. BIS Publishers.

National Highway Traffic Safety Administration. 2024. "Additional Information Regarding EA22002." April 25. https://static.nhtsa.gov/odi/inv/2022/INCR-EA22002-14496.pdf.

Nielsen, Jakob. 1994. "10 Usability Heuristics for User Interface Design." NN/g, last updated January 30, 2024. https://www.nngroup.com/articles/ten-usability-heuristics/.

Noble, Safiya Umoja. 2018. *Algorithms of Oppression: How Search Engines Reinforce Racism*. New York University Press.

Norman, Donald A. 2013. *The Design of Everyday Things*. MIT Press. First published as *The Psychology of Everyday Things* in 1988.

Norman, Donald A. 2004. *Emotional Design: Why We Love (or Hate) Everyday Things*. Basic Books.

O'Neil, Cathy. 2016. *Weapons of Math Destruction: How Big Data Increases Inequality and Threatens Democracy*. London: Penguin Books.

Parush, Avi, Shir Ahuvia, and Ido Erev. 2007. "Degradation in Spatial Knowledge Acquisition when Using Automatic Navigation Systems" in *Spatial Information Theory: COSIT 2007* [Lecture Notes in Computer Science 4736]. Springer. https://doi.org/10.1007/978-3-540-74788-8_15.

People + AI Research. n.d. "Datasets Have Worldviews." Accessed April 11, 2025. https://pair.withgoogle.com/explorables/dataset-worldviews/.

People + AI Guidebook. n.d. "Mental Models." Accessed April 11, 2025. https://pair.withgoogle.com/guidebook-v2/chapters/mental-models/.

Reference List

Pew Research Center. 2024. "Most Americans Favor Legalizing Marijuana for Medical, Recreational Use." March 26. https://www.pewresearch.org/politics/2024/03/26/most-americans-favor-legalizing-marijuana-for-medical-recreational-use/.

Placani, Adriana. 2023. "Anthropomorphism in AI: Hype and Fallacy." *AI and Ethics 3*: 1–10. https://www.researchgate.net/publication/377976318_Anthropomorphism_in_AI_hype_and_fallacy.

Reeves, Byron, and Clifford Ivar Nass. 1998. *The Media Equation: How People Treat Computers, Television and New Media like Real People and Places*. Cambridge University Press.

Restack. 2025. "Action Oriented Vs Result Oriented." Last updated March 13, 2025. https://www.restack.io/p/goal-oriented-agents-answer-action-result-cat-ai.

Russell, Stuart J., Peter Norvig, and Ernest Davis. 2010. *Artificial Intelligence: A Modern Approach*. 3rd ed. Prentice Hall.

Rutinowski, J., S. Klüttermann, J. Endendyk, C. Reining, and E. Müller. 2024. "Benchmarking Trust: A Metric for Trustworthy Machine Learning" in *Explainable Artificial Intelligence (xAI 2024)*. Springer. https://doi.org/10.1007/978-3-031-63787-2_15.

Schillizzi, Corinne. 2023. *Human-Machine Learning: Using Feedback to Design Systems That Serve Humanity*. Self-published. https://www.amazon.com/Human-Machine-Learning-Feedback-Systems-Humanity/dp/B0CLH1YP92.

Schumacher, E. F. 1973. "Small is Beautiful." *The Radical Humanist* 37, No. 5: 22.

Shneiderman, Ben. 1986. *Designing the User Interface: Strategies for Effective Human-Computer Interaction*. Addison-Wesley/Pearson.

Singh, Ashudeep, Yoni Halpern, Nithum Thain, Konstantina Christakopoulou, Ed H. Chi, Jilin Chen, and Alex Beutel. 2020. "Building Healthy Recommendation Sequences for Everyone: A Safe Reinforcement Learning Approach" in *Proceedings of the Workshop on Recommendation in Multistakeholder Environments (RMSE 2020)*. https://www.ashudeepsingh.com/publications/facctrec2020_singh_et_al.pdf.

Skalse, Joar, Nikolaus H. R. Howe, Dmitrii Krasheninnikov, and David Krueger. 2022. "Defining and Characterizing Reward Hacking." *arXiv:2209.13085*. http://export.arxiv.org/abs/2209.13085.

Reference List

Solon, Olivia. 2011. "How a Book About Flies Came to Be Priced $24 Million on Amazon." *Wired*, April 27. https://www.wired.com/2011/04/amazon-flies-24-million/.

Springer, Aaron, Victoria Hollis, and Steve Whittaker. 2018. "Dice in the Black Box: User Experiences with an Inscrutable Algorithm." *arXiv:1812.03219*. https://arxiv.org/abs/1812.03219.

Sweeney, Latanya. 2013. "Discrimination in Online Ad Delivery." *Communications of the ACM 56*, no. 5: 44–54. https://doi.org/10.1145/2447976.2447990.

Thaler, Richard H., and Cass R. Sunstein. 2008. *Nudge: Improving Decisions about Health, Wealth, and Happiness*. Yale University Press.

Toreini, E., et al. 2020. "The Relationship Between Trust in AI and Trustworthy Machine Learning Technologies" in *Proceedings of the 2020 Conference on Fairness, Accountability, and Transparency*. https://dl.acm.org/doi/abs/10.1145/3351095.3372834.

van Rijsbergen, C. J. 1979. *Information Retrieval*. Butterworth-Heinemann.

Vashney, Kush R. 2022. *Trustworthy Machine Learning*. Self-published.

Vincent, James. 2019. "AI Won't Relieve the Misery of Facebook's Human Moderators." *The Verge*, February 27. https://www.theverge.com/2019/2/27/18242724/facebook-moderation-ai-artificial-intelligence-platforms.

Vincent, James. 2020. "OpenAI's Latest Breakthrough Is Astonishingly Powerful, But Still Fighting Its Flaws: The Ultimate Autocomplete." *The Verge*, July 30. https://www.theverge.com/21346343/gpt-3-explainer-openai-examples-errors-agi-potential.

Wikipedia. n.d.-a. "Black Monday (1987)." Last modified February 5, 2025. https://en.wikipedia.org/wiki/Black_Monday_(1987).

Wikipedia. n.d.-b. "Pink Slime." Last modified February 7, 2025. https://en.wikipedia.org/wiki/Pink_slime#2012_controversy.

Willis, Lauren E. 2020. "Deception by Design." Loyola Law School, Los Angeles Legal Studies Research Paper No. 2020-25, 34. *Harvard Journal of Law & Technology 115*. https://ssrn.com/abstract=3694575.

Reference List

Weizenbaum, Joseph. 1976. *Computer Power and Human Reason: From Judgement to Calculation*. Freeman.

Welch, Jack, and Suzy Welch. 2012. *Winning*. New York: Harper Business.

Zou, Lixin, et al. 2019. "Reinforcement Learning to Optimize Long-Term User Engagement." *arXiv:1902.05570*. https://arxiv.org/abs/1902.05570.